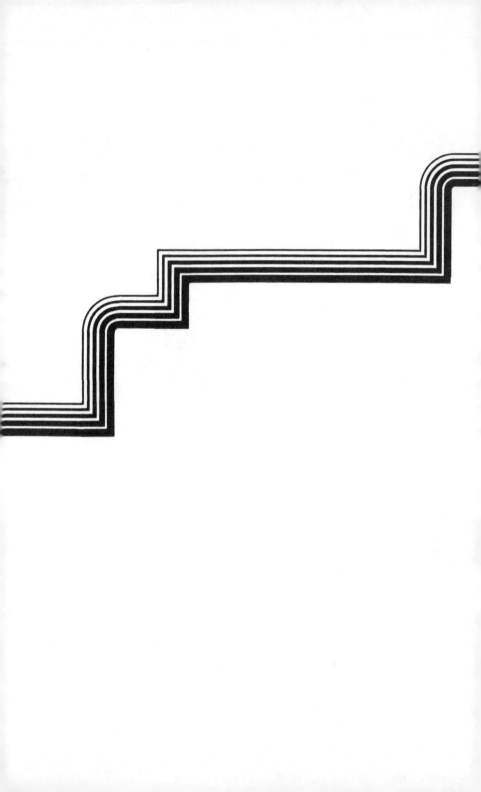

BY THE SAME AUTHOR

The Homeowner's Complete Guide

Do-It-Yourself Home Protection

Early American Furniture
You Can Build

How to Make Your Own Recreation
and Hobby Rooms

The Complete Book of
Basement Finishing

The All-Around,
Indoors-Outdoors,
Spic-and-Span,
Car-to-Couch,
Super-Hygienic,
and *Universal*

BOOK OF
With Other

A SUNRISE BOOK • E.P. DUTTON • NEW YORK

Upstairs-Downstairs,
Garage-to-Living Room,
Shiny-Bright,
Diamond-to-Doorknob,
All-Inclusive

CLEANING

Household Aids

by Ralph Treves

To My Wife
Estelle
with whom it's a pleasure
to share the cleaning chores

mation contact: E.P. Dutton, 2 Park Avenue, New York, N.Y.
10016 Library of Congress Cataloging in Publication Data
Treves, Ralph. The all-around, upstairs-downstairs, indoors-
outdoors, garage-to-living room, spic-and-span, shiny-bright,
car-to-couch, diamond-to-doorknob, super-hygienic, all-inclusive and universal book of cleaning, with other household aids.
1.House cleaning. 2.Cleaning. I.Title. II.Title: Book of cleaning.
TX324.T73 648'.5 78-17290 ISBN: 0-87690-238-7   (cloth)
0-87690-239-5 (paper) Published simultaneously in Canada by
Clarke, Irwin & Company Limited, Toronto and Vancouver
Designed by Barbara Huntley   10 9 8 7 6 5 4 3 2 1   First Edition

Contents

Introduction
How to Clean

This book was designed to serve as a ready reference to enable you to deal effectively and safely with specific cleaning problems that occur in and around the home, help make routine cleaning and laundering easier, and provide other pertinent information on household problems.

Cleanliness is a subjective concept, totally in the eye of the beholder. The time and effort expended by individuals on housekeeping chores vary considerably, of course; some confine their involvement to the proverbial "lick and a promise"; others conduct an intensive, ceaseless war on dirt, content with nothing less than squeaky clean. Most homemakers, however, manage to maintain sparklingly clean homes yet leave time for other interests.

Brilliant engineering advances in recent decades have greatly facilitated almost every aspect of housekeeping and household cleaning. New synthetic fiber textiles resist soil and staining; cookware coatings make washup a snap; plastic laminates for furniture surfaces and countertops are virtually impervious to damage or soiling. Paints and coated wall coverings are scrubbable, keep their new look almost indefinitely, and some lacquer-coated metals stay brightly polished without further attention for long periods.

Important also are improved laundering detergents and the many other efficient cleaners, of which there are special formulations for almost every purpose and material. New model vacuum cleaners are more versatile and efficient, while stronger kitchen exhaust fans, air conditioners and air filters help keep dust and grease at a minimum. Special-purpose brushes, synthetic sponges and scrub pads, treated dustcloths and similar tools, all help speed housekeeping tasks.

Technology rates applause for the development of the pyrolytic self-cleaning oven and the similarly porcelain-coated continuous-cleaning oven, thus eliminating one of the most time-consuming household tasks. Other manufacturers are making their products easier to clean by avoiding sharp bends in pans, putting on thicker electroplated coatings that stand up under repeated scrubbings, and providing for disassembly of appliances—essential for cleaning electric can openers, toasters and so on.

The flow of new products, however, presents difficulties in selecting the correct cleaner or tool for a specific function, and in using it properly. The problem is acute when dealing with plastic articles—what works fine on one type of plastic may well be damaging to another—although this problem has been eased somewhat by improvements in manufacture of plastic products.

While applauding the efficient new products, let us not forget grandmother's cleaning methods, tried and proven over generations. Many of these old-fashioned home solutions are emphasized in this book because the materials are readily available in the kitchen cupboard, are highly effective and economical, and are safe to use. The results achieved with vinegar or baking soda, even plain table salt or lemon juice, at times compare favorably with what the most sophisticated cleaning agents can do.

The alphabetical arrangement of subjects in this book, with cross-references where they apply, will enable you to find the needed information rapidly. Product brand names are supplied in some instances where such identification may be helpful; this does not imply that mentioned brands are superior to similar products that may not be named.

Readers are urged to give adequate attention to safety in

using and storing any product. Some cleaning chemicals are highly flammable and even explosive; others may be toxic or highly poisonous. In any event, be sure to pay attention to the warnings against cleaning methods and substances that rub off protective enamels and other coatings, cause scratches in utensils and appliance surfaces that make further cleaning impossible, and affect the colors or durability of garments.

The cleaning techniques described in this book were derived from various sources: the literature of government departments, the Home Economics Departments at Cornell University and the University of Florida, interviews with officials of national trade associations and the research technicians of product manufacturers, plus trial-and-error experiences of the author.

The oft-repeated instruction "wipe with a sudsy cloth" must seem to be a glib understatement, but cleaning is an everyday repetitive routine, and it's fortunate that most situations require no more than the typical swipe with soap and water. It is not the intention of this book, however, to brush off, or make light of, the very important household tasks that often—too often—require lots more than just a damp cloth to do the job.

How to Use This Book

The specific cleaning problems that you are likely to encounter in your home are arranged by subject in alphabetical order for quick access to the needed information. Related subjects that are covered more completely under other headings are cross-referenced to provide the additional details without needless duplication.

With certain categories that have been found to fall more conveniently into groups, such as *Automobile Cleaning,* you will find the data under that general heading, while each of the stages in the sequence is listed individually in a subheading—such as *Vinyl Tops, Whitewall Tires,* and so on. *Stains* also are grouped, with each type of stain individually listed under that general heading, including its method of treatment and solvents. Readers will find important suggestions for avoiding accidents grouped together under *Safety at Home.*

Laundering, one of the most frequently performed and complex household tasks, deserves a separate section, which you will find at the front of the book, together with informative sections on tools for cleaning and on soaps and detergents.

PART ONE
Making It Easy

Tools for Cleaning

The art of cleaning requires use of the most efficient tools for each task. Much progress has been made in improving the capability and quality of domestic cleaning aids so that they do their jobs more quickly, more easily and often better than before. Housecleaning, of course, hasn't reached the automation stage, when all it takes to get the work done is to push a button, but keep in mind that not so long ago homes were kept immaculately clean with just a dustcloth, a broom and a Bissell carpet sweeper—plus, perhaps, a service staff of two or three—an auxiliary that nearly all of us have learned to do without.

Nowadays, a well-stocked utility closet goes a long way to assure a clean, pleasant home, though there's plenty to do keeping windows sparkling, nursery furniture scrubbed, floors shiny, silverware polished and pots and pans spotless, as well as the stove, refrigerator, dishwasher and other appliances. Closets need to be dusted and their contents rearranged, bedding freshly aired, carpets and rugs vacuumed, sofa cushions fluffed and walls cleaned.

Knowing about all the cleaning aids and the recent improvements that have been made can be very helpful. These cleaning tools, in turn, need proper cleaning and maintenance so they'll continue to serve dependably. The following descriptions are provided to assist you in making the selections that will best meet your needs. Remember, though, the greater the capability of a tool, the less labor and trouble it takes to work with it. Besides, better-quality tools nearly always last longer. Put the two factors together and they obviously support the view that an additional initial outlay for a quality tool soon pays for itself.

The requirements for taking care of a large home are certainly different from housekeeping needs in a studio apartment, but strangely enough, both homemakers will require many of the same cleaning items.

THE TOOLS YOU NEED FOR HOUSECLEANING

Broom and floor brush
Brushes (radiator, scrub, toilet bowl, Venetian blind)
Buckets, at least two
Carpet sweeper, hand or electric
Chamois
Dishcloths
Dustcloths, treated polishing cloths
Dustpan, with extension pole
Floor polisher, with wax applicator and carpet shampooer
Mop, sponge or string type
Rubber gloves
Rubber kneeling pad
Scouring pads (copper, nylon, plastic, steel wool)
Sponges (cellulose)
Stepladder, 3-foot
Vacuum cleaner
Window squeegee

Broom: Wash a corn or fiber broom in warm water and detergent, rinse and hang on wall by the handle, straw end down, until completely dry. A small screw-eye in the end of the wooden handle enables you to hang up the broom easily.

Carpet Sweeper: Empty the dust collector pans regularly. Spread newspaper on the floor, open the dust pans by pressing the levers at each side and empty them; fold up the paper and discard. The sweeper brush eventually becomes clogged with entangled string, hair and cotton lint, which must be removed. Try gripping the string with a crochet hook, or cut the threads with a pair of scissors, then comb them out of the brush bristles. In some models, the brush can be taken out of the sweeper for cleaning.

Chamois: An expensive item, but it will last indefinitely when properly handled, and is well worth the cost in its performance. This soft leather absorbs a phenomenal quantity of water, is perfect for drying washed cars and windows. After using, wash the chamois in detergent water, rinse thoroughly, squeeze out the water, then stretch it to full size and place it on a flat surface to dry. Do not wash chamois with soap.

Dust Brushes: Soak in warm water with detergent, scrub the bristles with another brush or with a comb, to remove lint, hair and threads that may have been picked up by the bristles. Rinse, hang to dry; do not lay the brush on its bristles, which would bend them out of shape.

Dustcloths: Treated lintless cloths speed the dusting routine, do a better job because they pick up and absorb the dust instead of scattering it to other surfaces around the room. Some treated dustcloths are cleaned by shaking them (in the open, but not out of the window!) but there are others on the market that retain their effectiveness after being washed up to 20 times or more.

You can make treated dustcloths at home by putting a few drops of oily furniture polish into a glass jar with a screw cap. The cover is essential because oily cloths may flare up when crammed into an open container. Rotate or shake the jar so the inside surface is coated with oil. Cloths put into the jar will absorb just enough oil to pick up dust and polish the surface. Or you can use a mixture of 1 tablespoon each of mild soap powder (or detergent) and ammonia, adding 2 tablespoons of linseed oil or good furniture polish. Store in a covered metal or glass container, large enough for several dustcloths. Wash cloths as they become soiled; re-treat in the container after washing.

The One-Wipe dustcloth, now made in softer and heavier form than previously, can be washed up to 20 times without loss of the treated chemicals, as can the Handiwipe. Another effective dustcloth is Lady Kozak, which has a fairly deep nap that lifts and holds dirt.

Helpful Aids: A metal pancake turner or putty knife may be used to scrape off chewing gum and other stubborn spots on a tile or wood floor.

A length of broomstick screwed into the handle of your dustpan saves stooping when you sweep the floor.

Mops

SPONGE MOP: Sponge can be removed from frame, sometimes by turning out the retainer screws. Squeeze and rinse in warm water and soap for normal cleaning. When the sponge head becomes stiff with accumulated wax and soil, no need to buy a new one—you can restore it to like-new condition by boiling it for 10 minutes. Replace the sponge if fragments have torn off.

STRING MOP: Made of cotton strands, the mop head can be removed for washing. Place it in the washing machine with soiled cleaning cloths or wash it in a pail with hot sudsy water; rinse it thoroughly and hang it to dry, strings downward. Clean the metal frame and handle with soapy water.

Scouring Pads: The major types of scouring pads are described below.

STEEL WOOL: with or without integral soap, in various grades (S.O.S., Brillo). Unless listed as stainless, steel wool pads become rusted after one-time use.

COPPER MESH: for toughest cleaning chores, stubborn spots in pots, ovens, range tops, outdoor grills. Won't rust, may be used many times for tough scouring tasks—walls, tiles, patio. (Chore Girl and Chore Boy are familiar brands.)

NYLON PAD ATTACHED TO SPONGE: for general cleaning in place of steel wool (Rescue).

COTTON TERRY CLOTH: treated with plastic resin and silica for abrasiveness.

KNITTED PLASTIC MESH (BALL MUFF): polypropylene ribbon. Use for Teflon, fine china, dishware, porcelain sinks, tubs; also, for vegetables and all delicate cleanup jobs. Gentle to hands. Rinse and reuse.

SCRUB PADS: The mesh bag in which onions and oranges are packed can serve as a pan scourer. Remove the stitching from top and bottom, fold the bag at the center and tie with string. The coarse mesh is very effective for scrubbing pots and pans.

Sponges: Amazingly tough despite their softness, cellulose sponges can be made to last almost indefinitely. Squeeze, but do not wring, to remove water. Use the sponges with any type of cleanser, except full-strength bleaches. Put sponges into the washing machine or dishwasher to restore to like-new freshness (but tie them down so the sponges won't block the drain), or sterilize them by boiling with a teaspoon of baking soda.

Soft and resilient, and marvelously absorbent, sponges come in various shapes and types, including large squares suitable for washing cars and scooped-out blocks that serve as handy soap dishes. They are excellent for both applying and removing makeup, smoothing still-wet plaster patches on walls, polishing shoes, washing your car's windshield and chrome bumpers—in addition to the traditional kitchen and bathroom uses. Because of their absorbent capacity, small pieces of sponge placed around the bottoms of potted plants help retain moisture and absorb overflow.

Cellulose sponges are made of wood pulp, with cotton or hemp fibers added for greater strength and density. The holes are formed by mixing salt crystals of various sizes with the raw materials, then dissolving out the salt after the sponge is formed to leave the spaces. Coarse sponges are made with large crystals; the fine-pore sponges are made with powdered salt or smaller crystals. The dissolved salt is then crystalized to perform its function again and again.

There are also, of course, natural sponges in a wide range of sizes up to the great 12-inch type suitable for car washing and similar tasks. Natural sponges are still preferred by many, though they have been largely displaced by cellulose sponges.

Vacuum Cleaners: This is one of the most capable, versatile and essential cleaning tools in the home. It has one important job to do—pick up dirt—and it does that as no other equipment in the home can, reaching into inaccessible corners, lifting and beating and fluffing to get the dirt out, leaving rooms not only superficially clean but also deep-down clean. (See *Vacuum Cleaner,* page 176, for more details.)

Window Cleaners: Rubber squeegee blades speed window washing. A single stroke removes the dirty water and dries the window. A threaded handle permits attaching poles of various lengths to reach window areas that would otherwise be inaccessible or require a ladder.

The average squeegee (Ardmore, Greenview) is 12 inches wide; narrower 6- and 7-inch widths are better for French windows and small Colonial panes, auto windshields, mirrors. Cellulose sponges used for wiping washed windows come attached to plastic holders to which wood poles are fitted as needed to reach higher areas. A chamois is the best means of drying windows; it won't leave lines or streaks.

It All Comes Out in the Wash: Laundering

There's much more to good laundering than just pouring some detergent into the machine and pushing a button, although one would hardly think so after reading about "carefree" garments made with the newest synthetic fabrics, or watching a television demonstration of some miracle cleaning agent that—*presto!*—all by itself restores a pile of muddy children's clothes to sparkling newness, does away with sweat stains and odors, and removes the dingy look that had spoiled your favorite slacks.

Many homemakers approach laundering far too casually, as anyone can observe at a community "launderette." You don't have to be a chemist or an engineer to do the wash properly, but it certainly would help.

Those with extensive experience in doing the family's wash may find that the techniques suggested here challenge long-accustomed methods, but the change may overcome some deficiencies and should result in fresher, cleaner linens and garments. Once you adopt the correct techniques, you'll follow the routine methodically for consistently good results. Home economists are quite unanimous in the view that laundering difficulties mostly result from inadequate equipment or failure to follow recommended practices.

It is possible, as has been demonstrated from the earliest times, to do the family wash on a riverbank, flailing the linens against rocks for hours on end. There's a better way, of course, and surely you want to utilize the most effective modern methods.

Helpful Products: The magic, all-purpose, easy-to-use cleaning compound that does a perfect job, without fuss or bother, is a delusion, the product of an advertising copywriter's imagination rather than that of a practical chemist. Cleaners vary in composition and effectiveness, of course, so good laundering requires proper selection and use of detergent or soap, with attention to such details as sorting of the wash load, the water temperature and water hardness, length of machine cycles, size of load, and pretreating of heavy soils and stains. Important also is the quantity—by actual measurement—of the detergent, "builder," bleach, fabric softener you use. The dryer requires attention for correct heat setting and timing, an anti-static additive and cool-down period, as well as prompt removal of wrinkle-resistant garments.

It is interesting to compare the operation of a commercial "steam laundry" with the home washing-machine process that serves the same purpose—doing the family wash. The "steam" part of the laundry name merely denotes an adequate supply of truly hot water (usually at 160 to 180 degrees F.) needed for both effective laundering and sanitizing of wash loads that come from diverse sources.

The commercial laundering process usually involves six steps and takes about one and a half hours. In contrast, the home washing machine is programmed to complete the cycles in 20 to 30 minutes, but of course there is not the same need for sanitizing that exists when multiple loads are laundered jointly. Sufficient chlorine bleach in the wash and the ultraviolet lamp of the drier will sanitize the household's clothing and linens adequately.

HERE ARE THE RULES:

Attention to these basic requirements will provide the best results:

Sorting: Group the laundry items according to color, type of fabric and the amount or kind of soil. Make a separate pile of white items, another of colorfast garments. Test the color-fastness of any doubtful clothes in this second pile by wetting a corner to see whether the color bleeds. Non-colorfast clothes are washed individually, except that those of the same color may be combined in one load.

All-white clothes may be washed together—cottons, nylon, polyesters, etc.—provided each item can stand the higher water temperatures suitable for cottons; otherwise, separate them as needed. Do not include any garments that have colored trim such as monograms, collars, cuffs, belts and other similar items unless the label indicates they are color-fast. (See *Graying,* below in this section.)

Repair any rips and tears to prevent further damage in the machine. Close zippers, empty all pockets, brush dirt from cuffs, turn permanent-press and knit garments inside out to avoid snagging.

The family wash might be separated into these groups: Basically, keep heavily soiled garments in a separate machine load; wash white garments separately from colored items. To further improve results, wash the following in separate loads:

1. White cottons and synthetics (polyesters, nylons): table linen, bed sheets and pillowcases, dresses and slacks, hand-kerchiefs, washcloths, white towels.

2. Slightly soiled colorfast garments: children's clothing, underwear, shirts, snowsuits; also plastic tablecloths (try damp mopping first).

3. Sturdy non-colorfast items.

4. Heavily soiled, muddy, greasy garments: jackets, pants, socks, caps.

5. Hosiery, silks, rayons, delicate lingerie, brassieres, laces. Hand wash with Woolite in cold water.

6. Permanent-press items: blouses, shirts.

7. Delicate fabrics: sweaters, woolen scarves, woolen shirts, socks. Hand wash in cool water or dry-clean.

8. Curtains and draperies. Keep separate for special treatment as required by machine or hand washing.

9. Rubberized fabrics: girdles, support hose, stretch bands.

Wash by hand in cool water and mild detergent or special solution. Avoid contact with petroleum products such as Vaseline, which can affect the elastic strands.

Presoaks: Heavily soiled clothing and linens will come out cleaner if soaked before washing to loosen dirt. Rinse away the loosened soil that may cause discoloration of other garments in the wash. Pour the prewash product (Wisk, etc.) directly on the soiled areas, rub the solution into the fabric and allow it to soak for 10 minutes or so. (For stain removal, refer to the section on *Stains*, page 158.) Shirt collars, cuffs and sleeves that are stained by skin secretions may be treated with an enzyme presoak detergent; these are safe for machine-washable fabrics, but do not use them on wool and silk.

Presoak also soiled (but not stained) white cottons and other washable white fabrics in a solution of ¼ cup of detergent to 2 gallons of hot water, then rinse before placing in the washing machine.

One complaint about the effect of prewash soaking is that it could change the color at the treated spot, which may be as objectionable as the stain itself. Spraying the entire garment, rather than just the stained spot, usually overcomes this problem.

Hard-Water Laundering: Your local water company will tell you how hard your water is; you can have well water tested by your state agriculture department or city water department. Water is considered hard if its mineral content exceeds 3.4 grains per gallon of calcium and magnesium. Satisfactory laundering requires chemical treatment of the water to eliminate minerals that inhibit the action of soap and detergents and cause residual scum that contaminates the wash water and may cling to the garments. All detergents contain at least one of the two chemicals intended to reduce the hardness of water. One type precipitates the metallic salts, the other keeps the minerals in solution. For hard-water conditions, use a greater amount of detergent, one-and-a-half times as much in some cases, to make up for the reduced capability of the detergent. See later discussion of non-phosphate detergents in *Soaps and Detergents* chapter, page 18.

Hot Water: A heater setting of 140 degrees F. should provide sufficiently hot water for home laundering. If your heater is not of large enough capacity, or its recovery rate is too slow to maintain the flow near the required temperature, conserve the available hot water by having the family avoid baths, showers or use of the dishwasher when the washing machine is being used. Insufficiently hot water will not launder properly and contributes to problems, including the graying of synthetic textiles.

Some "cold water" detergents are effective mostly for lightly soiled items, when thorough cleansing is not required, for sensitive colors and delicate lingerie, and for woolens and silks that should not in any event be subjected to hot water.

It would appear desirable to equip washing machines with a gauge that would show the temperature of the water entering the machine, for better control and so that conditions causing a precipitous change could be observed and corrected. Appliance manufacturers evidently do not regard this as necessary, but it is a measure that they should consider as a means of improving home laundering facilities.

Size of Load: Keep the loads small enough to fit easily into the machine tub; avoid packing clothes tightly around the agitator. Put in larger items first; mix with smaller pieces by placing the additions around the center post so the clothes can move. Bulky items, such as a comforter, may be too large for the machine and may possibly be damaged by the agitator action. Loads containing permanent-press garments should be kept smaller than usual to avoid wrinkling. Machines with small-load baskets and water-level controls permit savings in hot water and detergent.

Overloading the washing machine can contribute to mottling the color of sprayed areas on garments because of uneven rubbing action; repeated laundering, however, sometimes restores uniform coloring. Soaking the garments for an extended period, several hours, for example, or overnight, can cause even a colorfast dye to run.

Enough Detergent? Don't guess—you may be shortchanging the wash load. Use a measuring cup to pour in the amount of detergent specified on the package. But the quantity is not inflexible—as mentioned above, increase the amount by as much as 50 percent to overcome the effect of hard water on the washing action of the detergent. An additional quantity also is needed when the load is larger than usual, contains permanent-press garments, or is more heavily soiled than usual.

Pretreating of heavy grease or oil stains helps retain the full strength of the detergent in the machine cycle.

Graying: It's distressing when T-shirts, cotton ducks and similar garments emerge from the washing machine white as snow, while certain nylon and polyester garments in the same wash have turned a dingy gray, and favorite garments are ruined. Happily, this condition occurs less frequently now with improved synthetic filaments used in the textiles. The prime reason for the graying of certain synthetic fabrics is the affinity of some fibers for the greasy particles in the wash water from dissolved soil lifted from the clothes. Some white garments are not truly white—the white comes from a fluorescent dye that washes out during laundering. There's no way to correct the yellowing that results from this.

Other causes of graying are:

1. Soap or detergent not thoroughly rinsed out
2. Bleach not neutralized
3. Load too large or too small
4. Too much or too little water
5. Water not hot enough
6. Alkali not thoroughly rinsed out

Brown discoloration caused by iron rust or manganese in the water source sometimes can be removed with a commercial rust remover made for fabrics.

To Restore Whiteness: Return discolored clothes to the machine, wash again, this time with the water as hot as the fabric can stand (adding boiling water from the range if necessary) and use more detergent. Polyesters and nylon, as well as cottons, can stand extreme heat. The following procedure is suggested by the Maytag Company:

Put twice the normal amount of detergent into the machine; allow it to dissolve. If the detergent is a nonphosphate type, add a water softener. Place clothes in the washer and agitate for 4 minutes. Dilute 1 cup of liquid chlorine bleach with 1 quart of hot water; pour around the agitator if the machine does not have a bleach dispenser. Restart the washer at once, let it run again for 4 minutes, then stop and allow clothes to soak for 15 minutes. Restart the washer, set for a complete wash and spin cycle. Repeat if necessary to restore whiteness. If a satisfactory result is not obtained at first, try adding a "builder" (phosphate) plus enzyme soak, and finally color removers. Whatever you do, however, the yellowing of certain fabrics cannot be reversed.

Labels: Clothing labels serve as a guide for sorting and machine settings, but they're not to be taken as rigid rules. You'll do better using your own discretion based on experience and special conditions. For example, the label on wrinkle-resistant garments specifies washing in warm or lukewarm water, but the most important factor here is not actual water temperature—a higher temperature is needed to get the clothes clean and to kill bacteria—but that wrinkling results from a rapid *drop in temperature* from the wash water of 140 degrees to a rinse of 120 degrees, or exposure to room temperature. The wrinkles become set in the thermoplastic textile at the time of a rapid temperature drop. In practical terms, the garments may indeed be washed in a machine at 140 degrees, but then should be transferred rapidly to a dryer with a moderate heat setting, just for a short time, then put on hangers for further drying, and wrinkles will be held to a minimum.

(Labels specifying cold wash, tumble dry, and moderate temperature, or calling for hand washing of sweaters, lingerie, woolen blankets and rubberized garments, should be closely followed. See also *Labels,* page 98.)

Laundering Permanent-Press Garments: These pose special problems, often requiring a compromise between the very hot water best for effective soil removal and the cooler temperatures needed for minimum wrinkling. The polyester fabric tends to maintain wrinkles if put into a spin cycle while the garment is still hot. The ideal solution is a cool-down period of the washing machine before the spin and rinse cycles. If this shift is not programmed for the washing machine, use warm rather than hot water, but heavily soiled garments will need separate laundering in hot water, and hand ironing.

Important for permanent-press garments is an ample amount of detergent and bleach in the wash. Pretreat grease or oil stains with full-strength liquid detergent. If permanent-press polyester knits become wrinkled after being left too long in the dryer, recycle in the dryer for 5 minutes on full heat, then cool down for 15 minutes.

Softeners added to the wash or rinse cycles—or to the dryer—reduce wrinkling and the static cling of synthetics and leave a coating on fabrics that softens them.

Men's Washable Suits: No longer the rumpled, sagging garments that were part of the summer scene, wash-and-wear men's suits now meet even meticulous style standards, retaining their shape and neatness after home laundering. It's a great convenience and money saver. Travelers can freshen a suit simply by dipping it into lukewarm water and hanging it up to dry overnight, carefully draped on a wooden or plastic hanger.

Make sure the label says "preshrunk." Before laundering, prescrub the collar with a strong detergent, pretreat stains, brush dirt from pants cuffs and empty pockets.

Bleach: Laundry bleaches help the cleaning process, preserve whiteness of fabrics, kill bacteria and deodorize garments. The two main types of bleaches—chlorine and oxygen—are available in both liquid and powder form. Most commonly used is liquid chlorine bleach, which works best in hot water. Chlorine should not be used on wool, resin-treated cotton, silk, acetates or spandex.

It is important to dilute the bleach, either by adding it to the machine after the water has entered but before the clothes are put in, or if poured in after the washing action begins, dilute with at least a quart of water. Do not pour the bleach directly on the clothes.

Oxygen bleach is milder than chlorine and can be used on all washable fabrics. Dry nonchlorine bleaches are gaining wide acceptance for laundering. They contain both sodium perborate tetrahydrate, a source of oxygen, and a percentage of sodium carbonate (soda ash) which provides additional alkalinity, converting the oxygen compound into hydrogen peroxide, the active bleaching agent. The dry form of this bleach permits incorporating other laundering aids such as surfactants (surface acting agents), water conditioners, brighteners, bluing agents and aromatic compounds in the formulation of a single, easy-to-use product. See also *Bleach*, page 42.

Sweaters: Whether woolen or of synthetic fibers, hand wash all sweaters in lukewarm water with one of the special detergents (Woolite, Cold Power), just squeezing the water through the material. Rinse several times, squeeze out excess water (don't wring) and roll the sweater in a dry towel to blot up as much water as possible. Lay the sweater on a towel to dry.

Nylon and Orlon sweaters do not shrink or lose their shape when drying. Wool sweaters, however, should be outlined before washing on heavy brown paper or cardboard so that they can be patted back into original shape while drying.

Soaps and Detergents

DETERGENTS:

Synthetic detergents are made from petroleum and natural fats and oils, to which are added various chemicals for specific cleaning purposes—builders, boosters, surfactants, corrosion inhibitors, bleaches and others. The detergents are basically of two types, light- and heavy-duty, but vary considerably according to individual formulas designed for the end purpose.

Detergents dissolve readily in hot or cold water, soft or hard. They do not form a scum in hard water, and the amount of suds can be controlled. Light-duty detergents, unlike soap, are nonalkaline and therefore are safe for silk, wool and dyed fabrics.

Heavy-duty detergents are the workhorse products for family laundering and general housecleaning jobs, but they also generally are safe for use on fine fabrics. The concentrated detergents contain one or more surfactants (surface acting agents)—ionic, non-ionic and catonic—which increase the wetting ability of the water by lowering surface tension, loosen and remove soil and emulsify oils (suspend them in the wash solution).

As a visual illustration of the wetting action of detergents, note that when clothes are placed in a washing machine in which detergent has already been dissolved in the water, they sink down quickly, while clothes tend to float in a machine that has only fresh water. To understand the esoteric chemical terms on some of the product labels, you need to know what the cleaners are made of, the purpose of these ingredients, and how they work. This will help you determine the actual differences between the various types and brands of cleaners.

Surfactant chemicals are essential elements of the detergent. The surfactant molecules pack in closely around the oily soil particles and lift them away from the surface, at the same time breaking up large oil droplets.

"Builders" in the detergent formula are usually phosphates which provide the alkalinity needed for adequate soil removal, control hard water by combining with the minerals (primarily calcium and magnesium) and act to keep the loosened soil in suspension so that it can be rinsed away rather than become redeposited on the washed surfaces. In the dishwasher, builders in the detergents prevent soil from combining with food particles that would leave insoluble spots on glassware, for example.

Another element is a corrosion inhibitor (sodium silicate) which helps prevent rusting of metal parts in the washing machine and preserves decorative patterns, such as gold leaf, on chinaware and glasses.

One important advantage in sticking with brand-name detergents and other cleaning products is that when you find one that is satisfactory, you can depend on later purchases of that product being of the same quality and having the same characteristics; also, you will have become familiar with the proper method for using it safely and effectively.

Phosphates: Do non-phosphate detergents perform as well as phosphate detergents? Yes and no. The carbonate powders (washing soda) do about as good a cleaning job under certain circumstances, says the Lever Brothers company. But they're not as good for cold-water wash or with colored fabrics unless the water supply is very soft—less than 3 grains of water hardness. The non-phosphate powders do not prevent formation of hard-water curds which may cling to fabrics, possibly causing stiffness and discoloration.

With heavy-duty laundry detergents, little if any difference in performance will be noticed when compared with phosphate cleaners under normal washing conditions. There are two ways to improve laundering results with non-phosphate powdered detergents:

1. Delay putting the clothes into the washer until the detergent is thoroughly mixed with the water—a wait of a minute or two—giving the detergent time to soften the water and precipitate out the water hardness minerals.

2. Use the hottest water suitable for the fabric. Hot water, ideally at 140 degrees F., minimizes hardness residue particles. A fabric softener like Final Touch helps keep diapers and towels soft. Wisk and All do not contain sodium carbonate (washing soda), thus are recommended by their manufacturer for washing flame-retardant garments and diapers.

SOAP

Soap is made by boiling animal or vegetable fats in caustic lye. Soap has the advantage of high alkalinity, needed for good washing; its chief drawback is that soap reacts with the minerals in hard water, forming an insoluble scum that tends to settle on clothes and give them an objectionable gray color. Some soaps (Ivory, Lux) are extremely mild, have a pleasant texture and scent, are smooth and come in attractive colors and shapes. Most people prefer soap for personal washing.

Heavy-duty soaps contain "builders" consisting of alkaline salts and water softeners to make them more effective in hard water. Soaps produce considerable suds, too much for use in washing machines and dishwashers. Most detergents do contain a limited amount of soap, but also usually include a suds depressant.

How can you dispose of suds that pile up in your sink? Sprinkle a teaspoon of salt and the suds will settle down. A cup of vinegar also will do the job, but that may work out as too expensive in contrast to waiting the few minutes for a suds-filled sink to empty.

How to Make Soap:

5 pounds fat (melted and strained)
1 pound lye (caustic substance, handle carefully)
1 quart cold water

3 teaspoons borax
1 teaspoon salt
2 tablespoons sugar
¼ cup ammonia

Use a Pyrex, iron or enameled pan. Dissolve lye in water, add the fat slowly, stirring constantly. Mix the borax, salt, sugar and ammonia together and add to the first mixture. Stir while heating over low flame until thick and light-colored; then pour into a wooden box or pan lined with cloth. Before the mixture hardens completely, score it into convenient-sized segments. When hard, break the pieces apart and pile them in staggered positions to allow complete drying.

Be careful when handling the caustic lye; avoid spilling on skin or clothing.

Part Two
Alphabetical Guide
to Cleaning

Acetone: Commonly present in homes as nail polish remover, acetone is the solvent for lacquer. It is used both as a lacquer thinner and for removing old lacquer coatings before respraying. Acetone affects certain synthetic fibers, particularly rayons and acetates. Acetone also is the solvent for rubber cement and it effectively lifts stains of ball-point pen ink. The chemical is highly flammable and should be used only with adequate precautions, preferably outdoors. Store in tightly sealed metal cans, except for small quantities in bottles needed for manicure purposes.

Acrylics: The exceptional properties that have put acrylic plastics into the forefront of the modern scene as cocktail tables, shelving, chair frames and backs, trays, drawer fronts and many decorative items, also include ease of cleaning and minimum maintenance care. Mostly, just wiping with a damp sponge or cloth keeps the plastic clean and fresh-looking; because of the smooth surface, sticky spots and stubborn

25

soil yield readily to a liquid detergent. Avoid dry abrasive cleaners and particularly do not use acetone, nail polish remover, or cleaning fluids containing benzene or alcohol that may soften the plastic. Ammonia and vinegar are safe cleaning fluids for solid acrylics.

Though exceedingly tough and durable, acrylics scratch fairly easily, so never use the plastic as a cutting surface. Protect tables from decorative metal objects by gluing tiny felt buffer pads where needed to prevent contact. Slight scratches are made less visible with a coating of wax. Deeper scratches can be buffed out with cheesecloth and paste cleaners like Brasso and Sudbury Gelcoat Cleaner and Waxer.

Non-toxic and non-conductive, acrylics are most widely known as clear, transparent materials. This plastic, however, can be tinted almost any color and is also available in milky white, translucent, or opaque. A special clear, shatterproof sheeting (Lexan, SAR, Lucite, Flex-O-GLAZE) is used for safety glazing of windows and storm doors—the latter required by many communities. Wash the plastic windows only with soapy water and ammonia or liquid glass cleaners that do not contain mineral solvents or alcohol. A coat of wax will help protect the plastic from the effects of wind-blown sand.

Solid acrylic parts can be joined together with a special, solvent-type cement that does not affect the polished edges of the parts that are joined.

Acrylics are thermo-plastic, sensitive to high heat and can be damaged by hot irons, close proximity to lamp bulbs (although the plastic makes attractive and practical lamp shades) and cigarette burns. See also *Lucite*, page 108.

ACRYLIC FABRICS: In fabrics, acrylic fibers are soft, fluffy, bulky, making them ideal for sweaters and other purposes. Acrylic fabric has good wrinkle resistance, yet retains original creases. In machine washing acrylic fabrics, use warm water and tumble dry at low heat. Use chlorine bleach after testing color. Examples of acrylic fabrics are Orlon, Dacron, (See also "Sweaters," under *Laundering,* page 17.)

Aerators: When water flow at the kitchen sink slows to a trickle, the fault may be clogging of the faucet aerator by sand and grit on the strainer screen. Unscrew the aerator from the faucet spout by turning it counterclockwise. No need to take out its screening and washers, as this may lead to complications in reassembling; instead, reverse flush by running water through from the outlet side at pressure.

When replacing the aerator, make sure that the threads are properly engaged with those on the faucet spout and that it turns smoothly and effortlessly; otherwise "crossthreading" will result and this ruins both the aerator and spout.

The aerator acts by mixing air with the water as it flows through, thus there is less splashing. The air is drawn in by vacuum through narrow slots in the walls of the hollow metal unit.

Aerosol Spraying: See *Automobiles: Paint Touch-up,* page 33

Air Conditioners: Keep your cool with regular attention to the air filters and condenser coils of your air conditioners. A clogged filter puts extra strain on the mechanism, increases the energy cost, and restricts the machine's performance. Insufficient cooling can also result from a coating of dust on the condenser or evaporator coils.

The filter is located near the air entry part of the machine. In a window-mounted machine, remove the front grill (on the inside of the house) either by lifting it to clear bottom lugs, or swinging the grill upward on hinges. The filter will be found directly behind the grill panel. (See *Air Filters,* below, for details on cleaning or replacement.) Never run the air conditioner without its air filter in place.

In a typical central cooling system, the filter will be found inside the blower unit, which is usually part of the furnace, located inside a special utility closet, or located in an attached garage. Lift off the removable metal panel. The filter may be held flat by a wire spring loop or metal band; lift this out of the way before withdrawing the filter, so that it does not tear.

Use the vacuum cleaner or a soft paintbrush to remove bits of leaves, insects, and cellophane scraps that may have drifted into the plenum space; also wipe dust from the condenser coils with a cloth. Be sure to disconnect the air conditioner electrical circuit whenever you clean the interior.

Typical central units include a plastic tubing, about 1 inch in diameter, which drains condensed moisture from the blower unit to outside of the house. This tubing must be flushed out at least once a year with a chlorine solution to prevent clogging. Unclamp the tubing from the machine, use a funnel to pour the solution of 1 quart of laundry chlorine bleach to 3 quarts of water. Replace the open end of the tube as before, carefully tightening the clamp to prevent a leak. If necessary, use a pail to collect the bleach solution as it drains from the outlet end of the plastic tubing.

Air Filters: Kitchen exhaust fans, air conditioners, hot-air furnaces and other home equipment contain air filters, which trap dust particles and clear the air of smoke, pollen, atomized grease and other foreign matter. Filters in time become clogged, lose their effectiveness and may allow dust or grease to enter air ducts and coat air conditioner coils, putting strain on the motor with resulting extra energy costs, possible breakdown of the equipment and potential fire hazard.

Types of air filters include the *disposable,* which are easily replaced with packaged fiberglass or charcoal filters, the *permanent,* which are washable for continuous use, and the *electronic,* which are self-cleaning. Frequency of washing or replacement depends on amount of use (as with the air conditioner) and environmental factors such as a nearby airport or busy highway that produces considerable soot.

1. *Permanent.* This type consists of a metal screening, a porous plastic sheeting, or a fiber pad. When removing the filter for washing, release any retainer clips to avoid tearing. Soak the filter for at least five minutes in hot water and detergent, flush under running water, rinse. It may be replaced while still damp.

2. *Charcoal.* Most consist of charcoal pellets in a cloth pad. If you have difficulty finding replacement filters, write to the manufacturer.

3. *Disposable.* Most are fiberglass in a cardboard frame.

For replacement, use the same type and model number as the original filter for correct fit.

4. *Electronic.* You probably remember from school days that when a plastic rod is rubbed on a bit of cloth it becomes electrostatically charged and attracts bits of paper. This basic principle operates in an electronic air cleaner to extract particles in the air as small as one-millionth of an inch, including tobacco smoke. In an electronic air filter, charging a filler of polystyrene foam causes it to attract and trap particles from air drawn over it by a fan. An aluminum screen retains the larger particles, and a layer of charcoal absorbs odors. Electrostatic filters can be installed into a forced-air heating system, or are available in individual cabinets. The screen and filter of these units are self-cleaning.

Filters are not to be confused with air fresheners, which come in various forms that function, essentially, by imparting a pleasant scent to overcome an unpleasant odor.

Alcohol Spots and Rings: See *Furniture Finishes,* page 82.

Aluminum Cookware: See *Cookware: Aluminum,* page 58.

Aluminum Siding: See *House Siding,* page 93.

Ammonia: The workhorse of household cleaners, ammonia is noted for exceptional grease-cutting capability. Household ammonia, basically ammonium hydroxide, now includes detergents, alcohol, salt and clarifying agents that improve ammonia's efficiency for light and heavy cleaning tasks.

For mirrors, windows, auto windshields, and glassware generally, use 1 tablespoon of ammonia to 1 quart of water. A stronger solution of ½ cup or 1 cup to a gallon of water serves for heavier cleaning jobs on bathroom fixtures, ceramic tiles, silverware, combs and brushes, barbecue grills, and cookware (but do not use ammonia on aluminum pots and pans as it will darken the metal). Vary the strength of the solution according to the job to be done, using fully concentrated ammonia for such purposes as deodorizing sink drains.

Apply diluted ammonia to the skin to ease the itching of poison ivy and insect stings.

Century-old Parsons' ammonia and other brands now

come in several varieties: *sudsy*—preferred for its quick action in cutting through grease and grime; not suitable for glass or mirrors because it may leave streaks; *clear*—best for windows, mirrors, stainless steel, porcelain; won't streak; *lemon*—a favorite everyday, all-purpose cleaner; perfect for kitchen and playroom as deodorizer; *pine*—powerful all-around cleaning agent; brings outdoor fragrance to closets, bathrooms, cabinets. Use a stronger solution to remove mildew stains on hard surfaces.

In laundering, add 1 cup of ammonia to the tub of hot water and decrease the amount of detergent—but not together with chlorine bleach. Blankets and woolens can be washed with diluted ammonia alone, without soap or detergent.

Caution: Never mix chlorine bleach or other household chemicals with ammonia, as harmful reactions may result. Ammonia is corrosive and poisonous if swallowed; antidotes are milk, diluted vinegar, orange and lemon juices. Do not induce vomiting; seek medical help. Wash off splatters of concentrated ammonia from the skin immediately and rinse skin with vinegar.

Appliance Bulbs: *See Lighting,* page 104.

Aquarium: Empty the tank for cleaning by pouring or siphoning off the water, after safely relocating the fish and plants. Wash the inside walls with a detergent or glass cleaner, then sanitize by swabbing the glass surfaces with salt water or chlorine solution (1 cup of bleach to 1 gallon of water). Wash the aquarium equipment at the same time and drain it completely—chlorine can be harmful to fish, so rinse everything thoroughly. Allow the tank to air for at least an hour before refilling with fresh water and returning the fish and plants.

A simple way to remove chlorine from tap water in the aquarium tank is with a little photographer's hypo (sodium thiosulfate). Just a tiny amount of hypo—equal to the size of an aspirin tablet—is sufficient to dechlorinate a 10-gallon tank of water.

Ashtrays: Empty ashtrays always into a metal container, preferably a "silent butler" type with hinged lid, making certain that all cigarettes are extinguished before discarding into the rubbish. Wipe trays clean with a paper towel dampened with rubbing alcohol to remove the gummy tar residue, or place in the dishwasher. An aerosol air freshener or the exhaust fan of the air conditioner will eliminate tobacco odor from the room. Setting out a few open bowls of vinegar also will do this perfectly.

Automobile Cleaning and Maintenance

ALUMINUM TRIM: Wash with mild detergent, rinse and rub on a protective coating of wax. Use metal polish to remove tar and stubborn spots. Avoid abrasives or caustic soaps on aluminum trim.

BATTERY TERMINALS: A white, powdery substance on battery terminals and cable connectors indicates corrosion. Wipe with a dry cloth and tighten the connector bolts. An inexpensive tool sold at auto supply stores cleans battery terminals to assure good contact. A heavier corrosive coating requires brisk brushing with a fiber bristle brush, never a metal one that could cause sparks and possibly explode battery gasses. Apply a coating of Vaseline or lube grease on the brushed terminals and cable connectors to prevent further corrosion.

While you're at it, check the battery's water; some new-type batteries have low-fluid indicators, others are sealed and never need refilling. If the fluid is too low, add distilled water, just enough to cover the top of the plates.

CHROME: Clean the chrome bumper, door strips and other bright metal parts of your car to maintain luster and prevent corrosion. A damp cloth usually is sufficient, but a concentrated detergent (Pine Sol, Fantastik) or a liquid metal polish may be needed to remove road film and tar. Use powder or other abrasives with discretion.

A wax coating helps protect chrome trim from dirt and salt-air corrosion. Clear lacquer sprayed from an aerosol can onto freshly damaged areas of the bumper or other chrome surfaces, provides a more permanent coating. Make certain the entire section is perfectly clean and dry before spraying. Remove the old lacquer with thinner when respraying becomes necessary.

CLEANERS AND POLISHES: The range of special cleaners for various automobile purposes is demonstrated by the DuPont Rally line, which includes all the following:

Cream Wax: in tube or jar form; the 8-ounce size is enough to do the car twice

Vinyl Top Cleaner: removes road film, grime and spots

Upholstery Cleaner: foamy type; for all soft interior surfaces

Vinyl Polish: self-polishing; for all vinyl, inside and out

Vinyl Dressing: wax formula; prevents cracking

Liquid Car Wax; with detergent-resistant silicones and waxes

Car Wash Concentrate: won't streak or remove wax; makes drying unnecessary (detergent)

Black Vinyl Top Wax: restores glossy shine, original color

No. 7 Auto Polish: the old-time favorite that still does its job with facility

New Car Wax: paste form, produces high gloss, long lasting

White Polishing Compound: moderately strong cleaner for removing weathered paint, traffic film, surface stains

Chrome Polish: cleaner and rust remover for bumpers and metal trim.

Tar Remover: solvent for road tar, oil, old wax; won't affect car finish

Tire Black: jet black paint applied with brush or wiped on

Engine Cleaner #3811: dissolves grease, oil, dirt, grime

Cooling System Cleaner #2131N: dissolves rust, cuts grease and scale (not for aluminum radiators)

Cooling System Flush #2212N: harmless to aluminum, rubber, etc.

Anti-rust #2412N: works in both plain water and antifreeze; safe for rubber hoses

Windshield Washer Refill #4013N: for automatic window washer tank; has antifreeze

Windshield De-Icer #3915N: includes scraper cap to remove ice

DuPont's Rain Dance: a group of auto chemicals including cleaner, polisher, vinyl top wax and body wax

ENGINE: Grease and dirt on the engine wiring can short out the high-tension ignition spark and prevent starting of the engine in damp weather. They also will cover up defective conditions and make servicing difficult. Clean the engine, including the spark plug porcelain, with any of the strong household detergents (Fantastik, Mr. Clean, 20-Mule Team), scrubbing with a stiff fiber brush. Kerosene and benzene are effective grease solvents, but are flammable and should be used with utmost caution. Avoid explosive gasoline. Steam jennies, a special motor-cleaning equipment used by shops that specialize in the process, make an engine look bright as new. There are also dozens of engine cleaners on the market that do a good job (Gunk, Heet, Rally, Duro De-Greaser).

Hard starting caused by jumping sparks can be overcome by spraying the coil, high-tension wires and distributor head with an ignition-waterproofing compound (Duro Ignition Sealer, Wire Dri, 4X Spray).

LICENSE STICKERS: The windshield inspection sticker issued with auto registrations each year must be scraped off before applying the new one. This can be quite difficult because of the close quarters resulting from a sharply sloping windshield. With a broad-blade knife (putty knife), first cut through the thick backing of the sticker. Place tissues or a towel above the dashboard to catch the paper shreds. If the ink coating of the sticker remains on the windshield, use a swab of cotton soaked with acetone (nail polish remover) to clean the glass. Finally, spray on a window cleaner to neutralize or remove the solvent before applying the new self-adhesive sticker.

PAINT TOUCH-UP: Scratches, stone chips, dents and other damage to the paint surface must be repaired promptly to avoid rusting of the exposed metal, which occurs very rapidly in some areas. Touch-up enamel or lacquer in aerosol spray cans is available from auto-supply dealers in the precise color to match the finish of your car, but keep in mind that there may have been some fading of the original finish, so the newly applied coating may be apparent, at least until it fades in like the rest.

Before spraying, sand the damaged area so it is smooth and the original paint edges "feathered" (that is, tapered); then wipe clean and dry. Do not paint outdoors on a windy day. Hold the aerosol can so its spout is 8 to 10 inches from the area; move the spout sideways as you press the nozzle lightly for just one quick burst. Wait until the first application dries hard before adding another very thin coat. Piling on too much paint at one time will cause lacy runs—wipe up quickly any that occur. Larger areas that need repainting should be left to commercial shops that are equipped with high-pressure sprayers, grinding tools and baking oven.

RADIATOR: Auto manufacturers generally recommend replacement every two years of ethylene glycol, "permanent" type radiator coolant. Alcohol and similar methanol-based antifreeze is more volatile, tends to boil away in hot weather; drain after each winter, adding rust inhibitor to the fresh water. Replace the antifreeze well before the start of freezing weather, then maintain the solution by hydrometer test at the level of freeze-up protection needed for the particular locality.

Accumulated rust and muck can clog the radiator, block water circulation and cause overheating. Commercial cleaners are usually effective, or you can make your own of equal parts trisodium phosphate (TSP) and washing soda in water. Pour this into the radiator, run the engine at idling speed for about 5 minutes or until hot, then drain. If this fails to restore radiator circulation, try reverse flushing—remove the engine port hoses, pack rags around the openings, and run water from the garden hose into the bottom outlet neck to float out rust scale through the top.

When draining the radiator, check all rubber hoses to see that they are in sound condition, securely clamped. Inspect also the fan belt for proper tension. Accumulated leaves and bugs trapped in front of the radiator's honeycomb may retard air flow for cooling the engine. Brush off the radiator front when washing the car. In certain months of the year, a soft plastic screen attached over the front grill will prevent clogging of the radiator by squashed insects and will help keep the air conditioner vents clear.

RUST PROTECTION: After each winter season, hose down the underside of the car to wash away salts and other corrosive chemicals used for road maintenance and ice removal. Particularly susceptible to this corrosive effect are fenders and doors, the fuel line, floor pan and exhaust pipes.

The asphalt-type undercoating of the chassis, done by commercial applicating firms, helps protect against corrosion, especially in southern areas that have very humid summers. This rust-proofing is not effective, however, where scratches of the surface finish, the paint or metal plating, have penetrated to the basic metal.

TIRE PRESSURE: The correct air pressure (pounds per square inch) of the tires varies according to the car's capacity and the temperature developed in extended driving. On the newer cars, recommended pressures are stated on a card attached to a door frame. Before starting on an extended trip where high-speed travel is expected, adjust tire pressure according to manufacturer's manual. When towing trailers, reduce allowable car load by the trailer hitch weight.

VINYL TOPS: Exposure to the sun's rays and environmental soot tends to discolor and dull vinyl car tops. Special vinyl cleaner wipes on fast and easily, dries to a rich gloss without buffing, adds depth and color that lasts for quite a while even in the rain. One such cleaner is Rain Dance brand. There are pigmented vinyl cleaners for use on colored vinyl, particularly the cabriolet decorative installations. A black vinyl top wax is available to renew the original gloss of the plastic covering.

VINYL UPHOLSTERY: There's a lot of vinyl fabric in every car these days—on the seats, door panels, roof top, dashboard paddings and the showy cabriolet body styling—so it's fortunate that vinyl is easy to keep clean. Go over the surface with a soapy sponge, wipe with a damp cloth and dry. Vinyl does not stain readily, so ice cream, coffee and other spills merely call for a little extra effort in the washup.

Rugged as it is, though, vinyl develops a lackluster, faded appearance on weathering. A foam-style cleaner, applied to a small area (2 square feet) at a time and scrubbed with a plastic pad or a soft-bristle brush, helps restore a near-new appearance. Do not use volatile solvents such as turpentine or acetone on vinyls.

Textile interiors are cleaned by methods explained in the *Upholstery* section, page 175. For leather seats and similar car fittings, refer to the *Leather* section, page 102.

When cleaning interior fabrics, in cars, stick to household detergents and spot lifters. Do not use acetone, carbon tetrachloride, enamel reducers, laundry soaps or bleaches. Never use gasoline or naphtha, which are extremely volatile and can cause flash fires.

WASHING: Just plain water, a sponge and some dry towels may well be sufficient for a once-over wash to keep the car trim and tidy. An all-around cleaning once in a while restores the crisp new look and interior freshness that prompt a sense of well-being for the occupants and the owner. The more thorough washing calls for a large sponge, a bucket of detergent solution, preferably special auto wash of which there are many satisfactory brands available, the garden hose and a chamois or a supply of terry cloth towels for drying. (DuPont puts out a car wash and sponge combination called Rally; there's also a phosphate-free wash concentrate that will not remove the wax and does not require drying.)

If the car has been standing in the sun, move it to the shade for a while, or start by sloshing lukewarm water from the pail, thus cooling off the car body gradually, before using the garden hose, to avoid excessively rapid temperature changes; the body metal expands and contracts at a different rate than the surface enamel.

Brush down the hub caps and bumpers first with detergent water; flush off the dirty water immediately. Next wash the body from the roof down, using the spray nozzle pressure of the garden hose while sponging off caked mud and film.

Continue with the doors, fenders, hood and trunk lid. Don't neglect the rocker panels below the door sills, which tend to become grimy with grease. Finally do the glass all around. After another thorough flushing with fresh water to remove any detergent, dry the surface with the chamois or towels, wringing them out as you go.

Road tar will show up on the cleaned car. Apply a few drops of linseed oil or a light household oil like 3-in-1. After the tar softens, wipe with an oil-soaked cloth, finish with a clean cloth. Special cleaners like DuPont Tar Remover are safe for car finishes of all colors.

A "dry wash" cloth, Kozak, will keep the car clean with a minimum of effort between washings. It is used only when the car is dry and cool. The soft, deep-nap cotton cloth is chemically treated to pick up surface dirt and grit, but sandy grit embedded in grime still can scratch the paint if rubbed in. Shake out the cloth to remove accumulated dust.

WAXING: Polishes and cleaners remove "road haze" and prepare the base for wax, which helps preserve the original finish. Apply the wax on a freshly washed car with a cloth pad, small sections at a time; buff with a soft cloth (or a cloth buffer pad on a power drill) until the wax shines. Simonize, DuPont's Rain Dance, Turtle Wax and Johnson's wax are well-known, dependable products.

WHITEWALL TIRES: Plastic soap pads, the kind used in the kitchen for scrubbing pots and pans, are best for cleaning whitewall tires. No need for a whitener—the white rubber will show through like new when the road grime and tar are scrubbed off—but you may have to use a scouring powder for a thorough job.

WINDSHIELD: A rubber squeegee does the quickest job of washing a windshield, but sends dirty water running down the side of the cowl, leaving streaks unless wiped up quickly. A damp chamois leaves the glass clear, without streaks. Window cleaners (Windex and Glass Wax sprays, DuPont Glass Cleaner Liquid and dry cake or powder cleansers like Bon Ami) are effective but require polishing with a separate dry cloth. A scrap of plastic screening wrapped around a sponge is handy for wiping off dried bugs and bird droppings.

Prevent fogging of your windshield by washing with soapy suds, or use a commercial defogger (Merex/Anti-Fog) which leaves an invisible film on the glass. Rubbing the inside surface of the windshield with a freshly cut piece of onion is said to effectively curb haze and steaming.

Awnings: Occasional flushing with the garden hose helps keep awnings fresh looking, brightens the colors. Canvas awnings will last longer if stored each year before rough weather sets in. Before taking down the awning, brush off dirt with a long-handled broom or spray with the garden hose. If the canvas is stained, scour with a laundry detergent applied with a hand or floor brush; rinse thoroughly. Finally, spray both surfaces of the canvas lightly with a mildew-inhibitor (Lysol, Listerine) from an aerosol can.

ALUMINUM: Enameled slat-style awnings can become dirty and discolored. Wash the stained area with a cellulose sponge and detergent or a paste type aluminum cleaner. When the finish of an enamel-coated awning or storm door becomes chipped, sand down the damaged area to the bare metal, then touch up the spot by spraying on an oil-base enamel to match the original color. Follow this method for aluminum windows and doors, house siding and lawn furniture with baked-on enamel.

CANVAS: Take down the awning by releasing the spring-loaded retainer clips. Do not let segments of the canvas sag without support, as the weight might start a rip. Lay out the awning on the lawn, fold into a bundle without compacting the creases. Wrap in kraft paper or a polyethylene drop cloth (you can buy this plastic sheeting in widths up to 12 feet, and rolls of any length). Store the bundle in a dry, well-ventilated place, preferably on a high shelf in the garage. Avoid piling heavy objects on top. The awning's pipe frame usually is left in place, but if there are signs of rust, protect with a coat of exterior-grade paint or a rust-inhibitor after sanding down to bare metal.

When setting up the awning each season, spread out the canvas on the lawn and inspect for holes or rips; it is easier to make repairs before the awning is erected. Cut canvas patches as needed, allowing at least 1-inch overlap all around, brush a heavy coat of contact cement on both the canvas and the patch, allow the cement to dry (about 20 minutes), then set the patch in place. The patch adheres instantly on contact, so place it correctly, starting at one end, letting it down gradually. Tap the patch with a hammer on a block of wood for adhesion. Double patches (one on each side) will assure strength. Complete coating with canvas-and-deck paint helps protect the awning and disguises the patch.

Before installing the awning, lightly oil the small pulleys so they turn readily. Set the canvas into position, tie the laces. If the awning has a gear box with rotating lift gears, lubricate it each season.

An efficient dry cleaner for canvas awnings is Rubgum, which is a porous cloth bag containing a very fine, grit-free powder. Squeeze the bag until some of the powder comes to the surface, and apply to the awning, rubbing the stain or spot as needed.

Bandage Tape: Although some manufacturers assure us that their bandage tape can be pulled off painlessly, more often than not the process involves a loud "ouch." Shaving the spot before placing the tape certainly would be helpful, but this is not always possible.

Another method that can be applied in certain circumstances is to spread a collodion coating over the area. Just a dab of the gel turns into a tough film that shields the skin from the pull of tape adhesive. Tape removal can be made painless also by applying a little isopropyl alcohol with an eyedropper along the tape edges, allowing it to sink in for a moment. Another tape-removal aid is trichlorofluoroethane, the same chemical in some dry-cleaner and spot-remover sprays.

Bathtubs: Daily spraying with a special cleaning fluid from an aerosol can or plunger pump bottle, and a quick wipeup with a damp cloth, will keep the tub always smooth and sparkling. An ingredient of these cleaners combines with and washes away the greasy "bathtub ring" that is formed by insoluble salts of hard water and is otherwise difficult to remove. Another effective method is to dissolve 4 tablespoons of Calgon in the bath water. The Calgon softens the water so soap lathers better, heads off any deposit of soap scum on your skin or the tub. (See *Calgon,* page 49.)

Occasional scrubbing of the tub will still be necessary. Swab a porcelain tub with a liquid all-purpose cleaner and a cellulose sponge—if kneeling alongside the tub to do this is difficult for you, use a sponge mop on a short wooden handle. For stubborn soil, rub with a mild paste or powder cleaner aided by some white vinegar or ammonia; avoid harsh scouring powders that can scratch the porcelain. Discoloration of porcelain yields quickly to an application of concentrated chlorine bleach.

(For care of fiberglass molded bathtubs, see *Fiberglass,* page 74; *Stall Showers,* page 168.)

BATHTUB AND SINK STAINS: Three types of stains are common on porcelain bathroom fixtures:

1. Blue stain, caused by a dripping faucet. Rub lightly with a plastic soap pad, then bleach discoloration with chlorine. If necessary scour with a mild cleanser such as Bon Ami. Stop the drip with a new faucet washer and, if necessary, a new washer seat.

2. "Rust" stain, due to iron in the water, usually brown or dark gray in color. Try lemon juice and salt, or chlorine bleach, applied with a sponge. If that fails, rub with a paste of moistened TSP with chalk, or try an oxalic acid solution (poisonous), one tablespoon of crystals to a cup of water on a sponge, and rub until the stain fades or disappears. Replace worn washers.

A special rust remover for use on bathtubs and sinks,

Whisk-Away, is claimed to be effective on iron rust and hard-water stains, without damage to porcelain fixtures. This product must not be used on fabrics.

3. Medicine stains from tincture of iodine, mercurochrome, Betadine, etc. Mix a paste of hydrogen peroxide and cream of tartar, apply to surface and allow to remain until it dries to a powder, then wipe away. Dissolved photographic hypo crystals (sodium theosulfate) and moistened perborate laundry bleach also are effective for removing medicine stains.

See also *Sinks and Bathtubs,* page 155; *Stains: Porcelain Fixtures,* page 165.

Battery Terminals: Make certain when installing any dry-cell batteries that the polarity is maintained; that is, the positive (plus) terminal and the negative (minus) terminal are in the correct positions indicated by a + or − on the unit. When not in use, store flashlight and similar batteries in the refrigerator to extend their "shelf life." For wet-cell batteries, see *Automobile Cleaning,* page 31.

Bamboo: See *Wickerware,* page 83.

Beer: Launder or dry-clean the entire garment if it is washable. Treat spills on carpet or upholstered furniture as quickly as possible with soap and water, rinse thoroughly. Follow with rubbing alcohol or full-strength vinegar to dissolve the sticky base and counteract the beer odor.

Rinse beer glasses after washing with diluted vinegar in the proportion of 1 tablespoon to 1 quart of water.

Bicycles: Polish with auto wax all enameled and chromed parts, including the wheel rims and spokes. Apply saddle soap (with lanolin) to a leather seat; use diluted liquid detergent on a vinyl seat. When bikes have become muddy, flush down with spray from the garden hose; dry with terry cloth toweling or a chamois.

Where the protective coating has become chipped or rubbed off, spray on a matching lacquer from an aerosol can, first masking all chromed parts with paper adhesive tape. (See *Automobile Cleaning: Paint Touch-up,* page 33.)

Oil the sprocket chain and wheel bearings once a month, or as recommended by the manufacturer. Remove tar and grease from wheel hubs with a solvent such as benzene.

Blankets

ELECTRIC: Do not dry-clean, as the solvents used will damage the wire insulation of the blanket. Hand washing is preferable, as described below, or follow directions provided by the blanket manufacturer. Dry on an outside clothesline, if available, but not directly in sunlight, or place in a prewarmed clothes dryer with the heater turned off. (Tumble dry.) Take out the blanket while it's still slightly damp and spread it on a flat surface to dry.

WOOL: All synthetic fiber and treated wool blankets can be either hand or machine washed at home. Hand washing is not too difficult and has the advantage of leaving the nap more fluffy. Drying is the main problem if outside clotheslines are not available, but this can be accomplished by tumble drying without heat in a clothes dryer.

Fill the bathtub partway with lukewarm water (100 degrees), add a mild synthetic detergent like Woolite, and soak the blanket for 5 to 10 minutes; swish the blanket through the water several times. Rinsing is the essential step: drain and refill the tub several times; each time swish the blanket around enough to wash out the suds. When the tub has been drained for the last time, squeeze the blanket to press out as much water as you can, but don't wring or twist it.

Start the dryer, let it run for a few minutes, then switch off the heater. Put in the blanket to tumble dry for 10 or 15 minutes. Include a few dry towels with the blanket to absorb some of the water and serve as a cushion. Remove the blanket while it is still slightly damp and dry it on a large flat surface. If necessary, the satin binding trim can be ironed. A soft brush can be used to restore the blanket's nap.

Bleach: Chlorine bleach is one of the most versatile and efficient cleaning aids. As a laundering additive, it removes stains, whitens fabrics, sanitizes and deodorizes clothes. It is effective also in general household cleaning and sanitizing of walls, floors, kitchen sinks, refrigerator interiors, toilet bowls, and garbage cans, as examples. It is invaluable in blocking mildew spores and removing mildew stains. No need to scrub Corningware and other porcelains—just pour in some full-strength chlorine bleach and the discolorations and stains will disappear.

Dry sodium perborate (oxygen-type) bleach is used when chlorine bleach would be harmful to fabrics. In machine washing it is not as effective as chlorine, particularly when used at low temperatures. The dry bleach is added to the machine load after the brighteners in the detergent have been allowed the few minutes necessary to do their work first.

Chlorine bleach or oxygen bleach must not be mixed with or used in conjunction with ammonia, as a toxic gas is produced.

CHLORINE BLEACH: Because of its superior cleaning and disinfecting ability, ease in handling and low cost, liquid chlorine is the most widely used bleach. This powerful cleaning agent consists of a 5 or 6 percent solution of chlorine (sodium hypochlorite) with a caustic soda (sodium hydroxide). The bleaching action is triggered by soil and organic matter in the wash, releasing hypochloric acid. The bleaching action is completed in just 2 to 4 minutes.

Granular (dry) chlorine bleaches contain organic compounds and are initially safer to handle but are not as effective for non-laundry purposes and are more expensive than the liquid type. They have largely been replaced by the oxygen-type dry bleaches.

Misuse of chlorine bleach will damage most fabrics. The usual dilution is 1 tablespoon to a gallon of water. Measure the correct amount, don't guess, following the instructions on the product label. A normal quantity for the average wash load is 1 cup of liquid bleach diluted in a machine load. The quantity is adjusted for specific conditions such as extra-heavy soil, restoring whiteness to grayed or yellowed garments, and prewash stain removal.

Best to dilute the bleach before pouring into the washing machine, and then only after the water has reached full level and all the clothes are thoroughly soaked. Allow a period of time for the detergent action to be completed, then pour the bleach around the pile of clothes, not on one spot, thus avoiding concentrated soaking.

Chlorine bleach should never be used on silk, wool or elastic fabrics, or on wash-and-wear garments that are colored with a resin that combines with and retains the chlorine so that the material becomes yellowed.

SODIUM PERBORATE BLEACH: The preferred dry bleach today uses sodium perborate, or hydrogen peroxide, as the oxidizing or bleaching agent. Because of its dry granular form, it is easily combined with detergents that contain other laundering aids like water conditioners, brighteners, bluing and perfumes.

Hydrogen peroxide is the chief component also of a liquid nonchlorine bleach, which has the limitation of not being compatible with alkaline builders.

See also *Laundering: Bleach,* page 16.

WOOD BLEACHING: Strip off old finish with paint remover. Let wooden furniture stand in direct sunlight to become heated, or place it under a photo floodlight to heat it. Apply full-strength chlorine bleach, wetting the entire surface. Add more bleach before it dries, until the base color is gone. Sponge off bleach with clear water, allow to dry in the sun, which is itself a strong bleaching agent. Finish by buffing with fine steel wool.

The white crystals of oxalic acid, which dissolve in water, are used for bleaching dark woods like walnut, and for removing inkstains. Sometimes used together with sodium hyposulfite in water solution, oxalic acid is poisonous and so should be used with adequate caution; wear goggles, rubber gloves and rubber apron.

Bluing: The practice of adding blue dye to the wash water, at one time a separate step in home laundering to improve the brightness of white fabrics, has been largely eliminated because most modern laundry detergents contain the dye. The bluing powder, if it is to be added, is first dissolved in water, then added drop by drop to the final rinse water until the garments are the desired tint. Avoid excessive soaking in the dye. If bluing has stained or streaked the garments, soak them in cold water, then run them through a second machine wash with warm water. When you wash blue denims and other dark cottons, extra bluing added to the starch will make the starching less obvious. Bluing has gained popularity of late for tie-dyeing and batik designing.

Bon Ami Polishing Cleaner: Made with feldspar, which has a hardness rating of 6, this cleaner cannot scratch glass, which has a hardness of 7. Bon Ami's mildly abrasive quality makes it effective for tasks where harsh cleansers are to be avoided, such as cleaning mirrors, ceramics, porcelain cookware and ceramic range tops. The cleaner contains a nonchlorine bleaching agent to remove stains.

The polishing cleaner comes in cake or powder form. It is moistened and applied with a gentle rubbing action. When dry, it forms a powder coating that assists the polishing step when removed with a soft cloth.

Books: Dusting with the circular brush attachment of the vacuum cleaner keeps books relatively clean without the need for removing them one by one to be dusted. Seasonally, the shelves should be completely cleared for a thorough wiping of both books and shelves. Inspect books for silverfish or other insect infestation; use the appropriate insecticide if necessary.

Leather bindings can be kept from drying out and cracking by an occasional wipe with a cloth treated with lanolin or castor oil; do not use mineral oil or other petroleum products on leather bindings. Cloth and vellum bindings should not be oiled, but rather cleaned where necessary with an art gum eraser. One cause of extensive damage to books is mildew; this can be prevented by adequate ventilation and maintenance of a normal humidity level in hot or damp seasons. (See *Mildew,* page 112.)

Vinyl and other imitation leather bindings are cleaned with mild soap and lukewarm water wiped on with a cloth, dried, then coated lightly with petroleum jelly to prevent cracking.

Borax: Widely used as a water-softening agent, borax also is favored as a mild cleanser and antiseptic, and is effective in retarding mildew spores and bacteria. A mildly alkaline salt, it is one of the chief ingredients in fire-retardant solutions. One interesting application: borax produces colorful flames when the powder is tossed into a blazing fireplace. Borax is used also as an additive in plaster of Paris to retard setting of the plaster up to half an hour and make the plaster harder.

Bottles: See *Glassware: Bottles,* page 87.

Brass: No matter how long it's been since your brass door-knobs were polished, or how black with tarnish and grime they have become, a few minutes of brisk rubbing with metal polish will restore them to sparkling brightness. This is true also of house numbers, electric switch plates, candlesticks and other brass items around the home, and a clear lacquer coating will keep them that way for months, even years, in most cases. Just plain lemon juice and salt, with flour added to form a paste, will do the trick nicely, but you'll find the task easier with a commercial copper cleaner having tarnish-retarding agents that keep the bright, polished look for longer periods. Labeled as copper cleaners, they are effective on brass as well, come in powder, paste and liquid forms.

Apply the cleaner with a sponge, felt pad or cheesecloth, using a discarded toothbrush for irregular surfaces and indentations. Rub briskly, in one direction only, for a minute or so until the bright color appears, then wash with a pad dipped in sudsy hot water, rinse and wipe dry. For a softer luster, rub with rottenstone powder dampened with salad oil or linseed oil. Rottenstone can be purchased at the cabinet refinishing sections of department stores, hardware dealers, home-improvement centers and mail-order houses.

A coating of clear or water-white lacquer is sprayed on from an aerosol can. Apply several very thin layers, allowing lacquer to dry at least an hour between coats.

Brass polish will not work on a lacquered surface; strip off the old coating by wiping with acetone (nail polish remover), the solvent for lacquer. (Acetone is extremely flammable; do not smoke while using it or expose it to flame.) The polishing can then be done immediately and a new lacquer coating applied when finished.

Well-regarded polishes include Cameo, Instant Copper Cleaner, Noxon Metal Polish and Copper-Brass Cleaner.

Smoke-blackened fireplace andirons may be somewhat more difficult to polish because of burned-on wood resins. Start with fine steel wool or emery cloth to penetrate the coating; the brass polish will then do the job neatly.

Breadbox: Vacuum clean or tap out crumbs frequently to avoid accumulation. Wipe interior with cloth dampened with white vinegar to keep it smelling sweet.

Bricks

PATIO: Bricks on a patio or terrace can be flushed down with a garden hose. If the bricks tend to crumble or chip, they can be preserved with a masonry sealer, which will give them a glossy appearance and smooth coating that makes cleaning easier. A coat of friction-resisting oil paint serves the same purpose and provides a desired color. The paint will, of course, require periodic renewal.

WALLS: Depending on how deeply dirt streaks or soot stains have penetrated the porous masonry, an adequate cleanup job can be done by scrubbing with TSP or a strong detergent and a steel-bristle brush. Paint splatters on brick usually yield to a paint remover—use the paste type, apply with a broad-blade putty knife and allow a couple of hours for it to soften the paint, which can then be scraped off. Two or three applications of the remover may be necessary to get at all the paint after the surface is removed, and some discoloration of the brick will remain. Try disguising this by rubbing with a piece of broken brick, preferably of the same color, thus grinding brickdust into the surface pores. The powder will be washed off in time by rain, but it's easy enough to repeat and eventually the colors will merge and become less noticeable.

Vertical white streaks on house brickwork may result from

"chalking" of paint on wood siding on an upper section of the wall. Chalking is normal and usually is so gradual that it does not affect the brickwork, but some paints deteriorate prematurely. This type of chalk discoloration usually disappears in time.

More difficult to overcome are the efflorescent streaks caused by the leaching of the lime content in the mortar of the wall. This condition is corrected only with a wash of diluted muriatic acid—a hazardous task that is best left to a commercial contractor. After the brick is restored to normal appearance, apply a coating of masonry sealer (PPG Speed-hide) to inhibit further leaching. Delay painting the brick until the wall is at least 6 months old—a delay for 2 years would be better—to allow time for weathering that washes away the uncured, powdery mortar and alkali salts that have come through the wall.

On brick and concrete-block walls, use a latex masonry paint. Walls that have been previously painted should be prepared for a new coating by removing any loose or flaking paint with a stiff-bristle brush—or if the condition is very extensive, sandblasting—followed by application of a surface conditioner as a base for the final coating.

Bronze: An alloy of copper, tin and zinc, bronze can be brightened with one of the special commercial bronze polishes, rubbed with a soft pad or cloth. Vinegar, hot buttermilk, rottenstone and whiting also are used for polishing bronze.

Butcher Block: Old-time cutting boards were made of maple sections laminated into a solid block with the cross-section grain as the cutting surface. After extended use, the surface becomes marked with knife cuts and nicks that trap food debris, presenting the danger of salmonella. Utmost cleanliness is essential. After each use, scrub vigorously with diluted chlorine and a stiff natural-bristle brush, then wash with baking soda and soapy water and rinse thoroughly. Do not use steel wool or apply oil, wax or other coatings. Periodically, sand the entire surface so it is smooth.

Mica-laminated and acrylic cutting boards are easier to clean with soap and water, but also may become badly scratched after considerable use. A ceramic countertop accessory by Corning is impervious to scratching, thus overcoming the objections to the other types.

Cabinets: See *Furniture,* page 81.

Calcimine: See *Whitewash,* page 182.

Calgon: This name for sodium hexametaphosphate combines the first three letters of the words "calcium gone" to describe the chemical's ability to combine with the calcium and magnesium salts of hard water, thus eliminating troublesome scale and scum, such as "bathtub ring," and helping soap to lather better. As little as ¼ teaspoon of Calgon in a quart of water is sufficient for removing discoloration from aluminum utensils, spot-free drying of glasses and silverware, and removing scale from the water reservoirs of steam irons. Calgon is tasteless and non-toxic, so it can be used safely for washing fruits and vegetables.

Calgon can be purchased at drug and hardware stores, supermarkets and mail-order houses, but is most commonly available as an ingredient of various cleaning agents. Calgonite is a separate brand name product containing Calgon that is formulated specifically for use in dishwashing machines.

Can Opener: The hand-operated type should be washed after each use, in the dishwasher or soaked in hot water and detergent, the cutter wheel scrubbed with a small brush to remove any residual food particles. Rinse and dry thoroughly to prevent rusting.

On some electric models, the cutter assembly can be lifted out intact for cleaning in the dishwasher or soaking in detergent. Be sure to disconnect the cord and pull off the magnetic lid catcher before cleaning. On other electric models, the cutting wheel can be taken off only by removing its retainer screw, a difficult job and one that can present a problem if the screw or one of the small parts becomes lost. Instead, clean the cutter by scrubbing vigorously with a small brush, then tip the whole case to overhang the sink so the top part can be flushed with hot water from the faucet, without wetting the motor section.

Candle Wax: Remove as much as possible with fingers, then scrape off the rest with a dull table knife. Wipe residue with benzene or paint thinner. Hot water will melt the wax and make it easier to remove from a surface that would not be injured by hot water.

Canvas Shoes: Put tennis and similar shoes into the washing machine with old towels for full hot water cycle. If heavily soiled, presoak in concentrated detergent solution. Air-dry to avoid overheating the rubber soles. Restore fresh new look with liquid whiting or commercial white shoe cleaner and whiting.

CANVAS SHOES WITH ROPE TRIM: Clean with foam type rug shampoo. Rub foam lightly with a soft-bristle brush or cellulose sponge. Avoid soaking. Wrap in a dry terry towel to absorb the moisture, then wipe with the towel, stroking in one direction to keep the fibers neat. Use spot remover as needed on soil or stains; remove chewing gum from sole with acetone. Caution: Flammable.

Carpets and Rugs: Frequent vacuuming or sweeping keeps carpets and rugs looking their best, removes the sandy grit that causes premature wear, destroys insect larvae. Shampooing or steam-cleaning at least once a year with the improved equipment and cleaning fluids now available removes embedded dirt and stains, restores the freshness of light-toned carpeting. A portable shampooing machine, rented by the day, uses specified detergents (Joy, Gleam), a spotting fluid (Carbona, Renuzit) or absorbent powder (Powderene, Glamorene, Sprinkle Kleen). When mixing the soap lather, use only the recommended amount of water so the carpet does not become soaked. Roll up the carpet, if you can, to clean the underside. (See also *Rug Shampooing,* below.)

Small cotton rugs can be put into the washing machine,

but first make a colorfast test. Don't dry-clean rubber-backed rugs that would be damaged by the petroleum solvent. Fiber and sisal rugs need only vacuuming. Reverse or roll up the rugs to get at soil that seeps through and collects underneath.

ORIENTAL RUGS: Periodic washing is recommended by experts in rug care, to restore the fine luster and colors. Once every second year or so, depending on location, is considered average care. The method of washing will depend on age, condition and type of yarn. Oriental rugs are quite hardy, can be safely washed at home. However, worn and delicate rugs, and those of antique silk, should be cleaned only by a reputable commercial service.

The first step in home washing is a thorough vacuuming of both sides, to remove as much dirt as possible. An old-time method used in colder climates is to do the cleaning in the wintertime when there is considerable fresh snow on the ground. After beating the rug vigorously for half an hour, turn it face-down atop the snow and leave it for several hours —dirty snow means cleaner carpet.

The actual washing is done either by flushing with plain water or applying a neutral detergent (without alkaline softeners or builders) such as Lux, Ivory, Woolite, Chiffon or Swan. Before washing, examine the rug for spots and stains, which must be removed before washing, or they may be spread wider by the cleaning action. Most water-soluble and solvent-soluble stains can be removed by home methods, but results depend on both the source and age of the stain. Spot removal also must be approached cautiously to avoid an incorrect method that may damage the yarn or affect the colors.

For water-soluble spots, soak facial tissues in water, place over the stain, with a clean porcelain weight to press on the tissue so it absorbs the staining material. For light spots caused by encrusted food and soil, try brushing while dry, then blot with a damp pad. Some stains, including those of coffee and liquor, may yield to soaking with fresh club soda, probably due to the fizzing action. Candy, sugar and milk spots sometimes can be removed by blotting with a damp cloth, which is rinsed repeatedly to flush away the contaminant.

Greasy stains are treated with a spot lifter, sprayed over the affected area and allowed to dry, then brushed lightly, hopefully carrying away the stain. Stubborn stains that do not yield to this treatment should be left to experienced commercial cleaners, called "spotters," to avoid possible spreading of the stain.

Small rugs can be washed comfortably at home in a laundry tub or similar container; larger rugs can be spread directly on a concrete surface, in the driveway or wide apron in front of the garage. Do the back first, spreading and working in the detergent solution with a brush; then turn the rug over to do the top the same way.

Rinse both sides thoroughly, using either the garden hose or buckets of water. Add half a cup of vinegar in the final rinsing buckets to bring up the bright colors.

Dry the rugs partially with terry cloth toweling, then hang them to dry. Small rugs can be placed over a clothesline, but larger ones may need to be supported across sawhorses or double clotheslines. Dry the back first, then reverse to dry the top surface. While still slightly damp, it's a good idea to brush the pile lightly to eliminate any creasing.

RUG SHAMPOOING: The process starts with careful spot-cleaning to reduce stains, then vacuuming to remove surface soil. The cleaning chemical produces strong fumes that are very troublesome to sensitive individuals, so windows must be kept wide open. All furniture is removed from the room (not just piled up in the center as for painting) and cannot be replaced until the carpet is really dry, which may take a full day or two, or even longer. Shampooing is a task that even commercial carpet cleaners may not do satisfactorily, leaving splotches of altered color.

You may achieve a modest result with a light going over, using a rented machine. Moistened powder containing sawdust and clay is brushed over the entire rug, then picked up with the vacuum cleaner.

SMALL RUGS: A cloth dampened with diluted white vinegar can help restore the bright colors of a rug. For cleaning, prepare a lather of 1 part mild detergent to 5 parts of water, whipped into foam with an eggbeater. Apply the lather to the rug, scrub with a stiff-fiber brush, rinsing each section as you go with a lightly moistened sponge. Work quickly to prevent water from soaking through onto the backing. Hang the rug on a line in an airy spot to dry.

"STEAM CLEANING": A portable machine, rented by the day, uses hot water—but no steam, despite the name—with a special liquid cleaner, and can produce a fine result, picking up ground-in dirt from deep in the carpet nap. Cost usually includes rental of the machine for a day or two, the stain remover and the special liquid cleaning product. The effort, though, is considerable, including picking up and returning the machine, shifting furniture, preparation of the carpet, filling and using the machine, then the cleanup. This is the usual schedule:

1. *Preparation of the carpet.* Vacuum clean to pick up loose dirt and objects like pins and staples. Search out any stains— with particular attention at entryways—and apply spot remover; allow it to seep in for at least 5 minutes. Clear the room of chairs and tables; place aluminum foil under the legs of large pieces of furniture to avoid discoloration.

2. *Assembly of the machine.* Fill the dispensing tank part-way with about 4 gallons of hot water, leaving a 5-inch space; add 8 ounces of the cleaning chemical. Pour a little water into the receiving tank, add defoamer to prevent sudsing in tank. Attach the vacuum hose and the solution line as required.

3. *Operation.* Turn on the pump and the vacuum cleaner; press the solution valve so the cleaning solution sprays onto carpet and the vacuum sucks the dirty water into the receiving tank. Do a small section of the carpet at a time.

4. *Refilling.* Empty the receiving tank when full; rinse. Refill the dispenser tank with hot water and cleaner.

5. *Disassembly.* Drain leftover water, disconnect hoses, return the machine. Allow carpet to dry (a day or more)

before replacing furniture and removing aluminum foil. Avoid walking on the wet carpet.

PROTECTIVE COATING: An application of Scotchgard, sprayed from an aerosol can, helps keep carpet fibers soil-resistant and water-repellent.

Casters: A common difficulty is binding of caster wheels by threads or hair caught in the wheel shafts. Use an awl or a small crochet hook to clear the shafts. Every 6 months or so, lubricate the swivel bearings of all your casters with a drop or two of oil to keep the wheels rolling smoothly. Wipe with a cloth to protect the floor from dripping oil. The newer nylon and offset metal casters (Shepherd) can go for longer periods without lubrication.

If a caster stem slips out of a leg when the furniture is tilted, the reason is a worn or spread retainer sleeve, the part that is recessed into the furniture leg. Wrap a couple of turns of tape around the caster stem, and tap back into the sleeve. Another way is to pry out the sleeve with a screwdriver or awl, compress the slotted end by slightly squeezing it with pliers, then replace and tap the bottom flange so the teeth around its rim sink into the wood. Insert the caster stem, pushing it in so the bulge at its top end bypasses and is retained in the sleeve. If the sleeve tends to slip out of place, wrap some tape around it for a snug fit.

You may be surprised to note how many casters there are in your home, most of them on bed frames, lounge chairs, nursery crib, typewriter stand, laundry hamper, luggage carrier, dinette chairs and other furnishings.

Centura Dinnerware: This is completely dishwasher safe, including patterns. Remove scorched-on or carbonized food by soaking in warm detergent water, then loosen soil with a plastic pad. Scour if necessary with baking soda or Bon Ami, using a wet cloth or sponge. Treat greasy soil with ammonia cleaner.

For cups with coffee or tea stains, soak in a solution of 2 tablespoons of chlorine liquid bleach to a cup of water, or overnight in 50 percent vinegar solution. Repeat if necessary with fresh solution, or use a similar concentration of dish-washer detergent. Brown discoloration from iron in the water system will respond to boiling in 50 percent vinegar solution followed by scrubbing with baking soda.

Chamois: Dries glass, windshields, car body. After using, simply rinse in clean water, or if cleaning is needed, wash with a mild soap in warm water. Do not wash with detergents, which would strip the oil from the chamois, making it white and stiff; do not store the skin when damp in a plastic bag, as the lack of air circulation will encourage mildewing. Stretch the chamois into original size and shape; allow to dry on a flat surface in the open air before storing.

Chandeliers: Take down the crystals, one by one, carefully straightening the soft hanger wires to do so. Wash the crystals in detergent; avoid chipping; dry with paper towels, the lint-free kind. The difficult task of removing, washing and replac-ing the crystals may be dispensed with by spraying an ionic cleaner (Crystal Safe) on the crystals from a plunger-type bottle. The sprayed solution dissolves dirt and grime, leaves the crystals sparkling. The chief problem is to prevent streak-ing; spray all surfaces of the crystals uniformly. Cover area underneath with a drop cloth or newspapers to catch and absorb dripping cleaner liquid.

Chimneys: Your heating plant will function more thriftily when the chimney is kept relatively free of soot by an annual clean-ing. It's not expensive to have the work done by a chimney-cleaning firm, but do-it-yourself cleaning need not be as un-pleasant a chore as is generally supposed. It's messy, certainly, and shouldn't be tackled if you're fastidious about getting sooty, or if you're allergic to dust. The job requires a wire furnace brush with flexible metal handle to loosen caked soot, and a good vacuum cleaner, preferably the canis-ter type used in home workshops.

   Make certain there's no fire in the furnace or fireplace. The first step is to take down the large metal flue pipe leading out of the furnace. It comes apart quite easily; just tap the joints with the palm of the hand. Place the flue sections on newspapers to collect the soot. With the brush, reach into the chimney as far as possible to loosen the soot, which will fall into an ash trap below, reached through a metal door. Brush out the trap into a metal pail after letting the dust settle; then reach into the chimney with the vacuum cleaner hose.

If a complete chimney cleaning is indicated, from top to bottom, this is done by dropping a sock filled with stones down the flue from above. Tied to a string, the sock is moved up and down, the soot falling into the ash trap. Before you do this, seal the flue opening near the furnace by bracing a piece of plywood over the opening; otherwise soot will fly everywhere. If climbing a ladder to the top of the chimney is a task for which you're not suited or equipped, it's best to turn the job over to a commercial firm.

Chromium: An occasional once-over with a damp cloth usually is sufficient to keep chrome-plated plumbing fixtures, bicycle handlebars, auto trim and similar items clean and bright. Always wipe dry after use to prevent water spots and to retain the fresh look. Various spots, usually from sulphur in the air, may require some rubbing with ammonia. Do not use scouring powder or any abrasive that may scratch or chip the chrome plating. Also, when changing a faucet washer or doing any other plumbing chore, protect chrome fixtures with masking tape wrapped around parts that are to be disassembled with tools. If the chrome has dulled a bit, any silver polish will shine it up, or just use ordinary white flour on a damp cloth. If the chrome is sticky with grease or from any other cause, wash with any metal cleaner, rinse, wipe dry with a paper towel.

Protect scratched spots on bumpers and other chromium steel auto parts with a coat of clear lacquer and wax to prevent rusting. Auto parts exposed to salt air near the shore, or to calcium chloride salts spread on highways in icy weather, should be flushed down frequently with clear water, washed often with soap and water, then waxed.

Coffee Makers: The way to get that elusive perfect cup of coffee every time is to keep the pot always perfectly clean, removing the traces of oils that make coffee bitter. Glass and ceramic pots are easiest to clean; stainless steel is a close second; aluminum and plastic are the most difficult. To clean, fill the pot with water to within 1½ inches of the top, cover and bring to a boil. Add one of the coffeepot detergents (dip-it, Mirro or Maid Easy), let stand for at least 15 minutes, or fill with water and a spoonful of baking soda. Wash with detergent, this time scrubbing the percolating tube and spout with a narrow brush.

The inside surface of a percolator or dripolator often becomes discolored from the coffee's natural oils or minerals in the water. This discoloration can be removed by scouring with a good household cleanser (Ajax, Cameo, Bab-O, or Bon Ami). To "sweeten" a coffee maker, fill with water up to the spout, add 2 tablespoons of baking soda and allow to boil gently for 10 to 15 minutes. Rinse thoroughly and dry.

The quality of the water is an important factor in the flavor of your coffee. Water that is heavily chlorinated or has a sulfuric odor can be purified to an acceptable degree by a filter, even the inexpensive compact type used directly at the sink connected to the faucet. A chemical water softener is most helpful, precipitating the lime.

Do not immerse the heating section of an electric percolator in water unless it's specifically designated as safe. Leave the coffee maker with top off when not in use, to allow air circulation.

Combs: Soak hard rubber, metal and nylon combs in baking soda or ammonia solution for 15 minutes, then scrub them with a small brush. Alcohol and Lysol also are effective cleaners and sanitizers. Nylon combs can be sterilized in boiling water, but not rubber ones. Run the teeth through a thread-type cotton comb cleaner to remove dirt and debris accumulated deep between the teeth.

Cookware: Pots and Pans

Thorough washing after each use is the easiest way to keep your cooking utensils in acceptable shiny-bright condition. A spot of grease or burned-on food can be quite easily removed while it's still fresh, but if allowed to remain, it becomes

carbonized during further cooking, and is much more difficult to scour away.

Most times, a quick once-over with a plastic soap pad (Rescue, Chore Girl), a dish detergent or cleanser and hot water
will do the job. More vigorous scrubbing, when necessary, is
accomplished with scouring powders and steel wool pads
(use stainless steel wool only, the other kind sheds bits and
quickly becomes rusted). Other effective scrubbers include a
bronze or stiff fiber-bristle shoe-polish applicator brush and
a coarse-textured nylon or copper-mesh pad. Some of the
methods used in former days, and still quite effective, include
a length of link chain wrapped in a dishcloth, crushed oyster
shells, and clean sand. The latter, excellent for scouring iron
skillets, can be obtained at masonry supply dealers.

ALUMINUM: Conducts heat quickly and evenly. Medium-gauge
extruded pans are best for general use; the cast types are
thicker, heavier, better for sauces and frying.

Scour with powdered cleanser and steel wool, inside and
out—except on polished aluminum where you should use
only a plastic or nylon scouring pad, moving always in one
direction to avoid cross-grain scratches. First soak pan in hot
water and detergent, or boil with diluted vinegar for 4 or 5
minutes, to loosen scorched food; then scour vigorously to
remove any carbonized spots.

Aluminum, whether cast or extruded, is subject to dents
and scratches that can harbor food debris and prevent
proper cleaning. Protect it from sharp metals or other objects
that can cause damage; avoid cutting food inside the pan
with a knife, and be careful not to cool a pot right from the
stove under the cold water faucet, as that can cause warping
(except in the case of heavy cast pressure cookers).

Darkening of aluminum pans results when one metallic
salt is plated onto a dissimilar metal. This occurs when foods
with iron content, such as spinach and oatmeal, are cooked
in an aluminum pan. But no need to laboriously scour away
the discoloration; when tomatoes, rhubarb, sauerkraut or
other acidic foods are cooked in the pot, the discoloration
disappears.

The lime scale that forms in tea kettles can be loosened by boiling vinegar and water, half and half, for 10 minutes.

Incidentally, it's difficult sometimes to know how much water is left in a boiling teakettle. One old-time method to keep the bottom from burning is to keep two small marbles in the kettle at all times—they'll rattle noisily when the kettle runs dry.

STAINLESS STEEL: Stainless steel pans can withstand scouring, but on any with a highly polished exterior surface use only a plastic or nylon-mesh pad and rub in the direction of the polishing lines around the perimeter, to avoid scratching.

COPPER: Many homemakers prefer to keep their copper pots and pans out in the open rather than hidden away in kitchen cabinets with the rest of the cookware, because they admire the attractive color and sparkle of the red metal. Copper, though quite soft, does not warp from rapid temperature changes, resists dents and scratches, and thus retains its unscarred smoothness even after many years of service.

A primary reason for the open display, very likely, is the ease of cleaning that keeps copper utensils gleaming. Numerous commercial copper cleaners do a creditable job; just a bit of rubbing with a plastic scrub pad removes food particles, flame marks and discoloration. Even burned-on carbonized spots on copper yield easily. Cleaning pastes can be prepared at home by mixing vinegar and salt, thickened with wheat flour, or combining powdered rottenstone with salad oil and some lemon juice.

Another attribute of copper for cooking is that heat is distributed uniformly over the entire base and is retained longer than with other metals after the flame is shut off.

What is generally regarded as copper cookware is mostly of aluminum or stainless steel clad with a copper base, as with Revere Ware, which utilizes the advantages of both metals.

You may have seen huge pots that are entirely of copper, a common sight in restaurants cooking spaghetti, for example, but those pots are fully lined with tin. Copper combines with acids in food, or even just with damp air, forming salts called verdigris. All copper salts are poisonous, so copper vessels are not suitable for cooking unless lined with tin, which is completely nontoxic and thus safe. But this lining may eventually be worn away by scouring or excessive heat. When this happens, a pot should not be used for cooking until relined by a coppersmith.

CAST IRON: Heavy, heats slowly, is subject to rusting (this can be prevented by greasing pan after washing). Preferred for frying and long, slow cooking. Wash with hot, soapy water, but do not scour. A little vinegar and salt boiled in an iron skillet loosens scorched food.

CROCK POT: See *Slow Cooker,* page 157.

ENAMELWARE: Absorbs heat quickly but unevenly; subject to chipping and stains from acids or excessive heat. Avoid sudden changes from hot to cold; allow pot to cool before washing. Cleans quite easily with soap or detergent, scrub with plastic pad; do not use scouring powder or steel wool. Rubbing with baking powder will remove light stains; chlorine bleach loosens stubborn food stains.

GLASS AND CERAMIC: Poor heat conductors but hold heat well and do not absorb odors or flavors. Can be taken from freezer directly to stove. When used on top of range they need a wire grid under the utensil. Encrusted food in casserole dishes is removed easily by soaking in warm water with a spoonful of baking soda. Stains in ceramic cookware magically disappear when soaked with concentrated liquid chlorine bleach.

BROIL PAN: In general, clean after every use in sink or dishwater. Let pan and rack cool completely, then wash in hot soapy water. Soaking in detergent with a few tablespoons of vinegar helps soften burned-on foods.

To clean a nonstick interior finish, wash regularly in hot soapy water with a nylon pad. Do not use a metal scouring pad or harsh scouring powder on nonstick finish. Clean the porcelain exterior finish and the broiling rack in hot soapy water with a nylon pad. Rinse thoroughly; otherwise discolorations will result when the pan is reheated.

To prevent scratching of the nonstick porcelain finishes,

store the pan in a vertical cupboard slot or cover with toweling. To remove stains or a mineral film, saturate a soft cloth with lemon juice or vinegar and rub over the finish.

NONSTICK PANS: See *Cookware: Teflon-Coated,* below.

TEFLON-COATED COOKWARE: Wash with hot, sudsy water, using a cellulose sponge or a rubber scrubber to loosen any residue of food or grease. No scouring is necessary. Never use steel wool, a metal scouring pad or scouring powder. While certain minerals in foods can cause discoloration of a Teflon-coated surface, this is harmless and does not impair the performance of the cookware.

The discoloration can be lightened with a perborate powder bleach (Sunbeam Teflon Cleaner) dissolved in a cup of water together with 2 tablespoons of baking soda. Simmer in the pan for 10 minutes at low heat to prevent boil-over of the suds, which would create a mess. Wash the pan thoroughly, dry with paper towels; "season" the inside of the pan with salad oil.

PYREX OVENWARE: The glass ceramic utensils can be put right into the dishwasher or washed by hand with detergent. Handles are detachable—make sure to remove them from the pan before placing in the oven. Here are important tips on how to use your Pyrexware to the best advantage:

Care in food preparation can make cleaning easier. If the recipe permits, grease baking dishes before adding food. This helps prevent sticking. Too much heat or too little liquid causes burned-on food. Follow recipes carefully for the correct ingredients and temperature settings.

To clean, begin by soaking in hot water with soap or dishwasher detergent. Then rub the dish with a mild cleaner, such as Bon Ami or baking soda on a damp cloth. If a scouring pad is preferred, use one like Dobie, Skruffy or Tuffy. Avoid using harsh scouring pads.

While Pyrex is dishwasher-safe, colors and decorations may fade or become dulled. Proper loading prevents dishes from rubbing against metal utensils, which causes gray marks that will require considerable effort for removal.

To keep food at serving temperatures, as in buffet service, use a warming tray. If a flame-type warmer is used, provide a flame spreader which has a metal plate that prevents direct contact of the flame with the dish.

PYREX RANGEWARE: Sticking food indicates cooking heat is too high. Avoid letting the water boil down completely, which weakens the glass and may cause it to shatter. Do not handle Pyrex cookware with a damp cloth; use a dry cloth or special handle. Clean with a plastic-mesh pad—do not use steel wool or abrasive powder. For greasy soil, use ammonia or all-purpose liquid cleaner with ammonia.

Pyrex rangeware, unlike the ovenware, cannot be used in microwave ovens.

PRESSURE COOKER: After each use, remove the pressure control weight from the cover and immerse the cooker in hot sudsy water to soften any encrusted food, then scrub the inside as needed with steel wool and soap. (Note: do not immerse electric heat-control cookers.) An enameled or color-coated exterior is cleaned only with a nylon-mesh pad (Rescue) and soap—do not use steel wool or any abrasive scouring powder on the outside surface.

Check the steam vent in the cover each time before you use the cooker by holding the cover toward the light to make sure it is not clogged. Clean the vent with a tiny rounded brush or a pipe cleaner.

There is also an automatic rubber air vent in Presto cookers that serves as a relief valve in the event the regulator vent pipe becomes clogged. This vent can be removed for cleaning by pushing it through from outside the cover. Wash in soapy water; replace by pushing it back from inside the cover —making sure it is properly placed with its slightly rounded face on the outside of the cover.

A dark discoloration that results from minerals in the water is harmless and does not affect the food. This stain may be removed, or lightened, by boiling a solution of 2 tablespoons cream of tartar to each quart of water, using enough to cover the discolored area. After boiling, allow the cooker to stand two to three hours, then drain and scour with a soap-impregnated scouring pad.

Periodically, every week or month—depending on the frequency with which the cooker is used—remove the rubber sealing ring for washing in hot soapy water. Before replacing, scrub the ring groove with an old toothbrush. The sealing ring is slightly oversized so that when replacing it, you must squeeze the sides together slightly, bit by bit, all the way around, to insert the ring into its groove. If not properly seated, the seal won't function and there won't be any steam pressure.

When the sealing ring is in place, coat its underside and the series of lugs on the metal cover with salad or cooking oil to facilitate opening and closing the cover. After extensive use the sealing ring may deteriorate and should be replaced with a new one obtained from the dealer.

A few safety measures must be observed: Never fill the pressure cooker more than two-thirds of its interior height, as certain foods expand when cooked and may plug the steam vents; when cooking rice, dried beans or vegetables, limit the quantity to no more than half full. Never force the cover open, and do not remove the steam regulator until the cooker has been cooled sufficiently.

TINNED COOKWARE: Excellent for baking, tinned bread and pie pans are easily cleaned but care must be taken to avoid scraping off the thin plated surface, exposing the iron base to rust. Soak if necessary to loosen food particles, scrub with a mild cleanser (Bon Ami) or very fine steel wool. Don't use scouring powder or other abrasive cleansers. Dry thoroughly before storing to prevent rusting.

Discoloration resulting from oxidation of the tin under high heat is regarded as providing the most favorable condition of the pans for baking.

Corelle: This tempered heat-resistant glass dinnerware by Corning is subject to scratching by sharp objects. Burned-on, scorched-on or dried-on food may be due to the cooking heat being too high.

Corian: This acrylic product, which resembles marble even to its delicate color tint and graining, has become widely favored for kitchen countertops, lavatory sinks and shower-stall panels. Occasional sponging with soap or detergent can keep Corian looking new and bright indefinitely. Stubborn stains and hairline scratches from knife cuts will yield to slight rubbing with a scouring cleanser (Ajax, Comet) followed by DuPont #7 rubbing compound to restore the high luster. Deeper scratches and other damage may be removed with fine (400-grit) sandpaper. Sanding with Wetordry sandpaper is recommended by DuPont, manufacturer of Corian.

Countertops: Although often subjected to hard wear and various forms of household soil, modern kitchen sink countertops are easily cleaned and maintained, keep their new look for many years. Most countertops are made of plastic laminate sheeting (Formica, Micarta, etc.) or ceramic tile. The former linoleum coverings, while very durable, were more difficult to clean and tended to swell up from absorbed moisture.

The laminated counters normally need no more attention than wiping with a damp cloth. Occasional food spots and other soil are removed with a sponge dampened with detergent, then rinsed with clear water. Avoid use of abrasive cleaners or coarse steel wool, as they scratch and wear down the plastic. Use chlorine bleach when needed, but sparingly. Also, do not let pools of water remain standing on the countertop even though the plastic is waterproof. Typical damage to the countertops are deep scratches caused by cutting food directly on the surface and scorched areas from placement of hot pans. A piece of plastic sheeting makes a convenient cutting board and can also serve as a spot on which to place pans hot from the range, although a metal or ceramic trivet would be better.

A recently introduced countertop material that has become popular is DuPont's Corian. Resembling marble in durability as well as appearance, it is warm to the touch and resilient, so there is less likelihood of breaking dishware. (See *Corian,* above.)

CERAMIC TILE COUNTERS: The white cement grout between the tiles is somewhat susceptible to staining. Scouring cleansers may be used safely for cleaning ceramic tile and the grouting. Cover the counter area with a paste of a foaming scouring powder (Comet) in hot water, allow to stand about 10 minutes, then scrub with a stiff-bristle brush and rinse. If stains still remain, apply undiluted household bleach for several minutes; rinse well and dry. After cleaning, the grout cement joints can be protected with a coat of silicone sealer. Repeat the treatment every 3 or 4 months to keep the grout free of soiling.

Crystal: See *Glassware,* page 87.

Cutting Boards: Wooden boards are fine for cutting bread and vegetables, but not so satisfactory for carving meats. The juices are absorbed into the wood fibers and cannot be readily washed away. A plastic board is more suitable. Specially formulated polystyrene or other plastic is odorless, waterproof and not affected by food acids or household chemicals —except acetone (nail polish remover). Simple washing with detergent or in the dishwasher will be sufficient. A ceramic cutting board is even better and cleans up more easily.

Dacron: A polyester fiber developed by DuPont from petrochemical compounds that are squeezed at high pressure through tiny holes to form a multifilament yarn. An important component of permanent-press garments, Dacron is favored also for lingerie, children's wear, curtains, blankets, carpets, sails and filters. Blended with other fibers, it is used also as filler material in pillows, comforters, and sleeping bags.

Dacron is tough, wrinkle-resistant, holds creases and pleats, dries quickly. In pillows it keeps fluffy after laundering.

See sections on *Laundering,* page 9, and *Permanent Press,* page 124, for care and cleaning information, or follow label directions.

Decals: Scrape off old decals from windows, auto windshields and similar hard surfaces with a single-edge razor blade or similar tool, then wash residual film with glass cleaner. On book covers, painted walls and other flat surfaces, soften the decal with sponge applications of hot water, or bursts of steam from a steam iron, then rub off the decal. If steaming is not effective, try an application of lacquer thinner (acetone), first scratching the decal a bit to allow penetration of the solvent so that it lifts the decal.

Dentures: Scrub with a special toothbrush having a high tufted end for reaching recessed parts. Ordinary bar soap is fine for daily cleaning; commercial denture pastes (Dentu-Creme) are slightly abrasive to remove stains. Efflorescent tablets (Efferdent) are effective cleaners. Always wash denture over a water-filled sink to prevent breakage if the denture slips. An electric sonic vibrator, with a special liquid detergent in a tank type container, removes food particles without abrasive action and does the best job of removing stains.

Diamonds: For the brightest sparkle, soak or boil diamond rings, pins, bracelets in diluted ammonia or white vinegar, then scrub with a toothbrush and soapy water to remove loosened grit or soil. Do not prod with a pin or other metal object to reach behind the prongs; that can chip the stone or bend the setting. If a ring or brooch contains other types of stones use the cleaning method suited to the most delicate stone; the diamond is the toughest of all gems and can withstand the most vigorous treatment.

Commercial jewelry cleaning preparations (Goddard Jewelry Care, Jewel Clean) sold by jewelers and most liquid glass cleaners (Glass Wax, Glass Plus, Spraying Glass Cleaner) effectively clean diamond jewelry.

Dishes: In the absence of a dishwasher, follow this cleanup routine that gets the job done with a minimum of fuss and in quickest time. Scrape plates and pans, wipe off grease with paper towels (helps prevent clogged drains), stack in sink or dishpan to soak in hot water and liquid soap or detergent, with a little ammonia added to cut heavy grease. Include the flatware and utensils used in meal preparation. Glasses, cups, saucers and bowls are rinsed and stacked to be washed separately, as they rarely need soaking.

Wash the dishes with a soapy sponge or plastic scouring pad (Rescue, S.O.S.). Once over lightly, top and bottom, usually suffices. If you have a double sink, place the washed dishes in the section on one side, filled with clear water. Drain and refill the sink for a clean-water rinse, then place the dishes in the drain rack.

Next wash the glasses, cups and cutlery with a soap pad or soapy sponge; if necessary to reach inside, use a narrow brush, such as the one for nursing bottles. Rinse under running water or in a water-filled sink. Dry the glasses first, then the flatware; finally the dishes, pots and pans.

PLASTIC DISHES: Plastic dishes and other tableware are subject to scratches; some also tend to become stained or change color. Wash with a liquid dish detergent; do not use steel wool or abrasive scouring powders. A homemade cleaning solution for removing heavy stains from plastic consists of equal parts bleach, baking soda and vinegar. There are several effective commercial cleaners and stain removers for plastic dishes such as Stain-aid, Dip-It, Maid-Easy.

Dishwashers: Use only special dishwasher detergents that are formulated to counteract water hardness, so the detergent can do its cleaning job, suppress suds, make water penetrate and loosen soil, emulsify grease, minimize spots by helping water to flow off surfaces, protect decorative dish patterns and inhibit corrosion of the machine metal.

An automatic dishwasher uses a relatively small volume of water. Contrary to what some people think, the dishwasher does not fill almost completely, as does a clotheswasher. The dishwasher, instead, employs several cycles, each with a relatively short water fill of only about 2.5 gallons, to accomplish the washing and rinsing operations. When water pressure is reduced at times because of other household demands, there may be insufficient water in the dishwasher. This can be avoided by curbing lawn-sprinkling, bathing and other like activities while the machine is in operation.

The temperature of the water is an important factor in the efficiency of the detergent and in removing food soils and drying the dishes properly (unless the machine has a heating Calrod coil). Water temperature should be 140 degrees to 160 degrees F. Water of this temperature helps sanitize the dishes. In hand dishwashing, the hottest water most people can stand is between 110 and 120 degrees F.

Load glasses and cups bottom up. Place flatware in the special containers. Large utensils should be placed in lower rack, glasses in the top rack, fitted into the wire retainers to stay in place under swirling water.

Gold-edged and hand-painted glassware or china that does not have a fired glaze covering the decoration should be washed by hand, not trusted to the machine unless specifically recommended by the manufacturer.

Plastic melamine tableware (this will be labeled as such on back of plates) can be placed in the dishwasher, but some other plastics must be washed by hand—polystyrene, polyethylene and other thermo-plastics (heat sensitive) are in this category. Hand wash also wooden utensils, anodyzed aluminum articles and sharp or pointed kitchen knives.

The dishwasher's interior is self-cleaning except that the strainer must be emptied when foreign matter accumulates; the door gasket, of vinyl or rubber, needs to be wiped clean occasionally with a soapy sponge.

The dishwasher will function best when used frequently, keeping valves and hoses in operating condition.

Disposal: See *Garbage Grinder,* page 86.

Doorknobs: The sparkling brightness of brass doorknobs and latch handles just doesn't stay that way very long because of tarnishing, even when the metal is coated with a protective lacquer. Tarnished brass knobs not only look drab and dirty, they tend to leave an unpleasant metallic odor on the fingers.

Polishing the knobs every month or so will keep the brass always looking its best, providing gilt highlights to the home's entrance and to all the interior rooms. No matter how old the brass, and how much service it has seen, a good polishing can restore an undamaged brass article to new appearance (see section on *Brass,* page 46).

Chrome-plated knobs and decorative door hardware need merely a light going-over with a damp cloth to retain the gleaming silver tone and remove any spots for a clean feeling to the touch. Where necessary, to remove a sticky or caked-on substance, wipe with a cloth dipped in a mineral solvent, such as kerosene or benzene (lighter fluid), or a fluid textile spot remover. Avoid using abrasive cleaners on chromed surfaces.

Down Jackets: See *Quilts: Down,* page 135.

Drains: Most drain clogs are caused by accumulated hair, grease, hard water scale or, in toilets, an object such as a medicine jar that falls into the bowl. The blockage usually occurs in the fixture waste trap directly underneath, at some sharp turn in the waste line, or it may even develop at the street sewer connection. The latter blockage affects drainage at all plumbing fixtures in the house and is more serious, possibly involving considerable expense. Clogging at one fixture indicates the trouble is at that fixture's trap or a nearby waste line.

The four ways to open a badly clogged sink or tub drain are:

1. Chemically, with washing soda or lye
2. With plunger pressure
3. With compressed air
4. Mechanically, by inserting a coil spring wire after removing the trap plug

Lye (sodium hydroxide) is commonly used to clear clogged sink drains. With a sponge, soak up all the water from the basin and as much as possible from the drain outlet; dissolve a can of lye in 2 quarts of water and pour this solution, which has become heated by the caustic lye, slowly into the sink drain. Allow the solution to stand for 10 to 15 minutes, then flush with clear water if drain has cleared. CAUTION: Handle the caustic lye carefully. Do not breathe in fumes. Mix only in a glass or stainless steel pan; avoid splashing on the skin or into the eyes.

A rubber plunger, called a "plumber's friend," is quite often successful. With the sink partly filled to provide an air seal, pump the plunger up and down over the drain opening for both suction and pressure, in an effort to free the blockage. The drain line has an opening to an air vent overhead so the plunger must be used in a way that puts on the pressure just at the moment when the water that has been forced upward is flowing back from the vent stack. Keeping this in mind, you will be able to determine the exact moment to press down hard on the plunger, forcing the water pressure onto the blockage. Another useful trick: lift the depressed plunger sharply off the drain—the resultant back pressure acts like a vacuum, exerting great pressure to loosen the clog. The latter "reverse suction" method frequently is successful in drawing out an object caught in the toilet trap.

Compressed air from a pump or an aerosol can is occasionally effective. Press the rubber cup at one end of the can against the drain to seal the opening while a blast of air is released to move the line blockage.

Mechanical action involves inserting a wire into the opening at the bottom of the trap after removing a screw-type plug. The auger type coiled wire has a handle at one end for turning to break up the clogging material, and should be long enough to reach the nearest bend in the waste line.

Clogging of sink drains can be prevented by periodic treatment. Dissolve 3 tablespoons of washing soda in very hot water and pour into the drain. Or place 1 tablespoon of lye into the drain with a cup of hot water and allow to stand a few minutes before flushing. Avoid putting solid matter, vegetable parts, coffee grounds and grease into the drain unless there is a garbage grinder. Empty the drain basket promptly.

Bathroom drains usually have a strainer to catch lint and hair. It may be necessary to release the drain plug rod (which opens and closes the drain) in order to lift and clean the strainer.

The overflow outlet built into a lavatory sink may become clogged from soap curds and other solids, voiding the protection offered by the secondary drain. A flexible spring wire pushed gently through the top opening may clear the blockage.

Drawers: Damp weather causes some drawers to balk. The cure is to coat the drawer sides, inside and out, with shellac so they'll be less subject to swelling from moisture, but wait until a period of dry weather before shellacking. Drawers that are sticky because of grit on the guide runners usually improve after a spraying with silicone type lubricant or with a liquid glass cleaner. Wiping with an ammonia-dampened cloth will remove old and grimy grease on the runners. Nylon rollers seldom give trouble and do not require lubrication, but the tracks must be kept clean.

Loose knobs or handles are corrected simply by tightening the retainer screws on the inside of the drawer. Don't try to tighten by turning the knob itself; rather, turn the screw at the back with a screwdriver, pulling it up tight.

Metal drawers, particularly those in filing cabinets, need periodic lubrication if the side rollers have ball bearings. A "dry" spray lubricant with Teflon (Elmer's Slide-All) or silicone type spray won't attract grime buildup.

Dyeing: A change of color can give a new personality to your old table linen, match up vari-hued bed sheets and pillowcases, or salvage a favorite gown. Almost any washable fabric can be dyed, and the process is done quite easily in washing machine or sink, but follow these rules carefully for a successful result.

The items must be clean—dyeing is not a substitute for laundering—and without spots or stains. The process accents rather than covers up any discoloration. The new color should be carefully selected: light colors come out best on white fabrics; stick to dark dyes when starting with deep grays, tans and browns. A solid color cannot be dyed over a print. Consider also what happens in color combinations—blue dye over red produces purple; a yellow dye on blue results in green—you surely remember about primary colors. (A more complete guide to color selection is offered by RIT Consumer Service. Address is listed in *Publications* section at back of book.)

For machine-dyeing, first dissolve the dye separately in very hot water, fill the empty washer with water and pour in the solution. Premoisten the garment, place it in the washer, which you've set for the longest cycle (for dark colors repeat the wash cycle before draining). Follow with a cold-water rinse. Put the garment into the dryer at medium-heat setting, except for woolens, which are always air-dried while flat.

Sink-dyeing follows the same basic steps but requires stirring with a wooden stick. Clean sink immediately when done, with bleach or wall detergent.

Dip-dyeing and tie-dyeing are fun and can produce very interesting effects. (RIT booklet on these subjects is listed in Part III.)

Elastic Garments: Girdles, support hose, surgical elastic garments, and some swimsuits contain Spandex yarn or latex rubber strands. Just rinse in cool water to freshen the garment after each wearing, or hand wash with a mild detergent. Jolastic solution, specially formulated for laundering elastic garments, assures excellent soil removal, prolongs the elasticity and contains a mild germicide.

Before laundering, close zippers, remove any fasteners. Rinse thoroughly, wrap in turkish towels and hang to drip dry away from heater or hot lamp. Do not dry in sunlight. Use nonmedicated talcum if necessary to dust tight garment for dressing. If bleaching of a stretch garment is necessary, use only sodium perborate, never a chlorine-type bleach. Do not allow an elastic garment to come in contact with grease or any oil-based medication.

Electric Irons: When starch and gum cause the sole of a steam iron to become sticky, run it back and forth over a sheet of paper on which salt has been sprinkled, or on waxed paper. Clogged steam vents can be cleared with a cotton swab or a pipe cleaner, and soapy water. Vinegar added to the water reservoir will clear up rust and corrosion in the iron. Fill the tank, let the iron become very hot, then drain the vinegar. Refill, this time using distilled water only.

Acetone (nail polish remover) will clean the sole of clinging synthetic fibers, rubber cement from adhesive tape, and most gums.

Electric Motors: Wipe lint and grease off the motor housing with a dry cloth—after the current is shut off, of course. Frequency of cleaning depends on location and the source of dust. Don't overdo the oiling of a motor: just 1 or 2 drops at each shaft bearing will suffice. An excess of oil will seep onto the commutator and brushes, may short out and damage the motor. Most appliance motors have sealed bearings that keep going without attention, often for a decade and more. If the seal begins to leak, however, the bearings must be oiled to prevent their burning out. Light auto engine oil, #20 or #30, is suitable for lubricating electric motors.

Exhaust Fan: See *Kitchen Exhaust Fan,* page 97.

Eyeglasses: Soft facial tissue, or a special silicone-treated tissue or linen, will keep eyeglasses clean, but occasional use of a liquid cleaner (Kodak lens cleaner) will do a better job. Dusty lenses should be rinsed in water before using a cloth cleaner, to avoid scratches.

Do not use the silicone-treated cloths or tissue on plastic "nonbreakable" lenses. These are best washed with soap and water, dried with a plain no-lint cloth or soft facial tissues.

Eye Hygiene: Bathe the eyes nightly, or when desired, with a solution of boric acid and water, or just by splashing water over the lids. Eyelash roots and eyelid margins are washed with mild baby shampoo, applied with a cotton swab and rinsed off thoroughly. When selecting eye cosmetics, give preference to the water-soluble type; buy small quantities at a time so they'll stay fresh; discard any more than 3 months old. Apply mascara to the tips of the lashes only; use glue for false eyelashes sparingly and wash it off each day.

Ferrotype Plates: Chrome-plated brass sheets, used for obtaining glossy photographic prints, tend to become coated with a chalky residue of gelatin particles. This causes sticking and damage to the emulsion of drying prints.

Apply Kodak liquid ferrotype plate cleaner or cake type Bon Ami (not the powder or spray form) with a soft cloth after a group of prints is dried, to remove residual particles. Bon Ami leaves a layer of fatty acid on the surface that prevents sticking of the prints.

Do not flush water directly on ferrotype plates that are fastened onto print dryers; rather, wash with a moist sponge, rubbing lightly, or use the ferrotype cleaner.

Fiberglass: Polyester-coated fiberglass bathtubs, vanities and shower stalls have come into wide use as original installations instead of the typical porcelain fixtures. The plastic fixtures, molded and installed as a single integral unit, can retain their attractive new appearance and colors for years with proper maintenance.

Use only liquid detergent or mild nonabrasive paste cleaners, never harsh scouring powders or abrasive pads. When the fixture is brand new, apply one or two coats of good automotive paste wax, rub in and polish by hand with a soft flannel type cloth. This will make subsequent cleaning much easier and help retain the high gloss of the fixture, but may make the tub slippery. That can be overcome by cementing friction strips to the bottom of the tub. Wax every 3 or 4 months.

When the surface becomes dull or has accumulated smudges, clean with an automobile type rubbing compound (DuPont No. 7, or Johnson's Auto Cleaner). Rub vigorously with a soft cloth or a felt pad, then wash with liquid detergent. Mineral solvents like benzene, turpentine or paint thinner (they're flammable) may be used sparingly, while some conditions may require buffing with an electric polisher. (See also *Bathtubs,* page 40.)

Chips or scratches in the fiberglass can be repaired with a special catalyst formula consisting of a specified quantity of gel coating obtained from the manufacturer of the fixtures. Thoroughly clean the entire area to be repaired to assure adhesion of the filler material; spread the material smoothly over the patch. Before the gel sets, cover with waxed paper for slow drying. Allow at least 2 hours for the filler material to set at average room temperature; remove the waxed paper, then rub the patch with very fine sandpaper to reduce the material so it blends in with the original surface.

Fire Extinguishers: It's good to have extinguishers at hand but don't count on them too much—they're not usually accessible when needed, they may not be in working condition at the time or of the right type for a particular blaze, and often they are of inadequate size to do the job. Experts agree it's better to get out of the house and sound the alarm than to lose time trying to fight the fire.

About the most dependable protection you can have is to keep an open box of baking powder in the kitchen to toss onto a fat fire in the stove. If you have chemical extinguishers, check the pressure dial at least twice a year, service them at once if needed, keep them accessible.

Receiving wider acceptance for the home is the automatic sprinkler, fitted into existing water lines. While a complete installation would be prohibitively expensive, even impossible in most existing homes, the sprinkler heads can be fitted onto exposed water pipes in the basement or laundry room. Sprinklers need no servicing, let loose a stream of water to douse a nearby fire when a thermal bar is melted by the heat. But weigh these advantages against the extensive water damage that results when a sprinkler goes into action.

Whatever else you do, be sure to install dependable smoke-flame detectors in appropriate locations in your home.

Fireplace: Clean out the fireplace hearth with sufficient frequency to limit fly ash in the room. Use the broom part of the fireplace set to brush dead ash into piles, first lifting the grate out of the way. Shovel the ashes into large grocery bags; close them tightly to keep fly ash to a minimum and discard properly so the bags are not torn.

With the vacuum cleaner, pick up the remaining fine ash, reaching the vacuum hose into the chimney rather than brushing down the ash, as that stirs up considerable dust.

Some areas are troubled by birds coming down the chimney and stirring up a storm of soot and noise. If a bird is trapped above the draft or behind the screen or glass doors of the fireplace, open a couple of windows and shut the room door, then open the draft and/or move the screen aside, providing a means for the bird to escape. Placing a heavy metal mesh over the chimney top will prevent birds coming down. (See also *Chimney,* page 55.)

FIREPLACE STONES: After the cold season when you're not likely to use the fireplace for months, the hearth interior can be washed if you don't like its sooty look. Soot-darkened fieldstone is cleaned by scrubbing with a strong solution of trisodium phosphate (TSP). If this doesn't work, it may be necessary to use muriatic acid in a 1-to-3 solution with water. Apply with a fiber-bristle brush and allow to remain on the surface for several minutes or until the bubbling of the acid stops, then rinse with plenty of clear water. Caution: wear goggles and gloves, as muriatic acid is a hazardous chemical.

BRICK FIREPLACE: A heavy-duty floor detergent, applied vigorously with a fiber scrubbrush, usually suffices to remove soot and other soil from a brick hearth. Deep discoloration of the brick may respond to a paste of coarse pumice and concentrated ammonia; allow to become thoroughly dry, then soak with a strong liquid cleaner and scrub. Some householders find that coating the front brick with a liquid wax—the kind used on vinyl floors—makes cleanup easier.

A handful of coarse salt thrown into a blazing fire is an easy and inexpensive method of burning soot off the fireplace walls. Some old fireplaces are built of ordinary wall-brick that deteriorates, while the mortar crumbles under the intense heat. A fireplace that has such openings in the hearth wall is a fire hazard. Rebuilding the hearth with firebrick laid in special clay mortar is advisable.

ANDIRONS: Remove discolorations on brass andirons by scouring with a copper cleaner and plastic soap pad; finish with a brass polish buffed to a golden glow. (See also *Brass*, page 46.)

Floors: First step for floor washing is to remove as much of the furniture as possible from the room to obtain a clear path and eliminate the need for shifting things around. Prepare two buckets, one with hot water and the cleaning solution, the other with fresh water for rinsing the mop or scrub brush as you go. For the washing solution use an all-purpose detergent (Spic and Span, Pine Sol, Mr. Clean, Soilax, etc.). Add ½ cup of sudsy ammonia.

Divide the floor area mentally into segments using various features of the room as guides. Do one segment at a time, first scrubbing with detergent, then rinsing; squeeze out the mop in clean water and rinse the washed area before going on to the next segment. Discard the dirty rinse water when necessary—the detergent should remain clear throughout. It is not usually necessary to wipe the rinsed floor absolutely dry (except for wood floors) unless traffic into the room cannot be restrained for the needed drying period.

Many homemakers prefer to scrub the floor on their knees with a fiber-bristle brush, and their efforts obviously are justified by the splendid results. Tiles with embossed surfaces or pattern indentations usually require this more direct scrubbing effort.

Waxing helps keep dirt from sticking to the surface, saves wear of the floor covering, provides an attractive, shiny surface, and not least, makes routine floor washing easier.

LINOLEUM: To clean a linoleum floor there are three essential steps: 1. Sweep up all the loose dirt. 2. Mop thoroughly with hot water and a detergent such Top Job or Mr. Clean. (Wring the mop frequently, so that there will not be too much water left on the floor). 3. When the floor is completely dry use an applicator pad on a long handle to apply a thin coating of Klear, or some other floor finish that is expressly designed for linoleum floors. One method of application is to pour a small quantity of the Klear into a shallow tin dish. Dip the applicator into the dish and smooth over the floor. Allow this to dry thoroughly before walking on the floor. The coating of floor finish will protect the linolem from heel marks, scratches and ground-in dirt, and will make it much easier to keep the floor clean and glossy with only a few light sweepings. If the wax surface turns yellow, be sure to remove all the old wax, mopping with hot water and detergent before putting on the new coating.

MARBLE: A coating of hard wax helps protect marble from absorption of dirt, makes cleanup easier. Wash by mopping with hot water and a detergent with ammonia. Heel scuffs usually respond to rubbing with a felt pad and powder cleanser; try a nonabrasive type first, resort to a stronger cleanser with scouring pad if necessary. Rub in a straight line only, with the grain of the marble if that is visible, but in any event, avoid circular motion that will leave marks.

Chewing gum can be removed with very fine steel wool after scraping with a broad knife. Don't use a sharp pen or paring knife that can leave scratches.

Floors showing discoloration or varied spots that do not wash off can be restored to bright freshness with an electric floor scrubber used with fiber or felt pads and special detergent. These machines can be rented by the day at local hardware stores.

MOSAIC TILE, TERRAZZO: Wiping with a damp sponge or mop is usually the only maintenance required to keep the floor clean. When a more thorough washing is necessary to remove stains, food spills, etc., use a solution of trisodium phosphate (TSP) or a soapless detergent (Spic 'n Span, Oakite) that won't leave a film. As the unglazed ceramic tiles age, a patina forms on the surface that gives a soft shine and keeps the floor fresh-looking longer.

QUARRY TILE: Occasional mopping with a diluted solution of soapless detergent (Spic 'n Span, Oakite, etc.) will keep the unglazed ceramic tiles in like-new condition. For heavy cleaning, scrub thoroughly with an all-purpose cleaner or powder (Mr. Clean, Lestoil, Top Job, Janitrol, etc.), covering stubborn soil spots with a paste of moistened scouring powder; allow to stand for 5 minutes or so, then scrub with brush or scouring pad.

NON-WAX VINYL TILE: Perfect cleanliness is the secret for keeping the lovely gloss of vinyl for years without waxing or buffing. Dirt, food spills, heel marks can be wiped easily off the slick surface; routine washing will keep the surface immaculate. Use a general-purpose detergent with a cellulose sponge to loosen and flush off dirt. Rinse thoroughly with fresh warm water—rinsing is an important step to avoid leaving a film that will hold tracked-in dirt. Do not use any abrasive cleaners.

Between moppings, sweep or vacuum the floor regularly to prevent dirt buildup. Take whatever steps are necessary to prevent abrasion, place a doormat at each entryway, use glides or plastic cups under furniture legs, install casters.

The tile may gradually lose some of its gloss over a period of time, depending on the extent of the traffic in your home, or the amount of abrasion from sand or other means. The glow can be restored by applying a special coating (Solarian Floor Finish by Armstrong). The floor must be absolutely clean so that dirt cannot be trapped under the new coating.

WOOD: There are many variations in wood floors, ranging from pine planks and walnut to birch, beech, pecan, oak and maple, and a wide variety of patterns including blocks, strips, and tightly fitted parquet. Some are cemented down, some nailed, others pegged, and the floors may be finished with varnish, oil, stain, urethane sealer, wax, shellac or deck enamel, each with its special cleaning and maintenance requirements.

Whatever kind of wood floor you have, there's one detail that applies: Wash with as little water as possible— even on wood that has a sealer coat or is painted. Never leave water standing on the floor, wipe spills immediately, avoid water-based wax and polishes. The purpose is to prevent water spots on the surface finish and possible warping of the boards.

Stubborn soil that clings to waxed floors can be removed by rubbing lightly with steel wool moistened with turpentine or similar solvent. For white water spots in a shellac surface, use a soft cloth saturated with alcohol, diluted 1-to-1 with water. Apply lightly; do not rub, to avoid cutting through the shellac surface. If that happens, however, see details on retouching below. When complete washing is necessary to clear food spills or tracked-in soil, use a detergent solution followed by a clear water rinse, in both instances using the smallest amount of water and wiping it up promptly. For an overall cleaning before putting down new shellac, always use a floor-polishing machine with a pad of No. 3 steel wool, then vacuum and rinse with clean water, sponged up at once.

When waxing, use the paste type, polished with an electric buffer, rather than the water-emulsion type.

Worn traffic spots on a shellacked floor can be touched up readily with shellac and will blend in perfectly. After a light sanding and dusting, apply the shellac in several very thin coats, each allowed to dry thoroughly and sanded with fine-grit paper to smooth out the pebbled surface.

Remove embedded soil from a varnished floor by rubbing with a mixture of pumice in lubricating oil and wipe with a solvent-saturated cloth to pick up sticky oil, which will collect grit.

For renewing a varnished area, first strip it down by sanding or with a chemical remover. Make sure that the touch-up coat matches the shade of the original.

Here's the test that will tell you whether a wood floor is coated with shellac or varnish. Soak a small piece of cloth or blotter with alcohol (rubbing alcohol will do) and place it on an inconspicuous spot for a few minutes. If the finish becomes softened and can be wiped up, it is shellac. Alcohol will not affect varnish. (See also *Painting: Paint Tool Cleanup,* page 120.)

WAXING: Self-polishing wax in liquid form, sometimes combined with a cleaning compound, is easily put down. Just a light buffing with a soft mop or cloth polisher brings up the desired shine. This self-polishing wax is not as permanent as the hard wax type, but is renewed readily on a newly washed floor without special stripping, as is the case with hard wax. The self-polishing wax is water soluble, therefore not suitable for use on wood floors.

Polishing wax in paste form, much more durable, is renewed by occasional buffing. The wax comes in light and dark shades, is best put down with an applicator, thus eliminating knee-action scrubbing. After spreading the wax, allow it to remain for a half hour or so for the thinner to evaporate, then buff with nylon pads in an electric floor polisher (can be rented by the day at supermarkets). Apply the wax in a very thin coat, or you will end up with a sticky surface that is difficult to clean. Waxes tend to become yellow after a time, giving the floor an undesirable cast; strip off the old wax before putting on a new coating.

Furniture: Atmospheric conditions in the home have an important effect on furniture. Excessive humidity can be responsible for intermittent swelling and the consequent balking of drawers, while the low humidity that often prevails in the winter months may cause drying of the natural oils in wood furniture, separation of glued furniture joints and dulling of the finish. Additionally, corrosive elements in the air of some regions may deteriorate metal furniture parts, particularly brass and plated items.

Drawers may be protected from moisture absorption with a shellac coating (see *Drawers,* page 71). Application of lemon oil to furniture replaces the oils that have dried out and restores the finish, which can be protected by a coating of wax.

The bright polish of metal furniture can sometimes be restored by rubbing briskly with a silver- or copper-cleaning paste, but if the corrosion has caused pitting of the surface, nothing but a machine polishing and buffing will do an adequate job. Protect metal surfaces with a coating of clear lacquer, applied from an aerosol can. The lacquer must be renewed periodically, every 6 months or even more frequently depending on the location and effect of the corrosion. Be sure first to remove the previous coating with lacquer thinner (acetone) wiped on with a cloth. (See also *Brass*, page 46.)

WOOD FINISHES: A simple application of lemon oil or other furniture polish can restore the brilliant gloss or patina of the wood. It is not always necessary to remove all the old wax when polishing, but this should always be done before waxing. Many furniture polishes contain solvents that remove the old wax, or at least thin it out so that the polishing achieves the essential objective—that of spreading out the existing wax. This brings up a chief detail: the tendency to put down too much wax, and very commonly, to pile up one coat upon another.

If a cabinet surface is heavily smudged, or the finish appears drab or discolored, wash with a light rubbing of an appropriate solvent (turpentine for wax, acetone for lacquer), then polish with fine steel wool and dust thoroughly. Allow to dry, then apply lemon oil or a similar finish like Liquid Gold—just a few drops on a felt pad or a handkerchief.

This treatment should bring up the original finish, accenting the grain and leaving a fine surface film that inhibits lint and dust. The protective coating of a hard paste wax then can be put down, very thin and well worked out by brisk polishing.

Select lemon oil that is free of additives such as linseed oil (which usually is sticky), beeswax or silicone, all of which are intended to produce a shine that is not always desired and can affect the finish adversely.

UNVARNISHED WOOD: Renew the finish of unvarnished walnut or teak with boiled linseed oil thinned slightly with turpentine and tinted with soluble stain, if desired. Allow the oil to seep into the grain for an hour or so, then wipe away the excess with a dry cloth. Rub the surface with a felt pad to work in the oil, then apply wax, or if you prefer, polish with lemon oil to obtain a natural, hand-rubbed patina. One decided advantage of the hand-rubbed oil finish is that if the surface is scratched, you need only apply more oil and rub it in.

Some wipe-on finishes, such as Lemon Pledge, produce an attractive luster with very little rubbing. An application usually eliminates rings, smudges and other discolorations.

CANE FURNITURE: Dulled chair caning can be revived by wiping with vinegar diluted with an equal amount of water. While still damp, rub to a shine with a soft cloth and allow to air-dry. For routine cleaning, brush with a saline solution, 1 tablespoon of ordinary salt to 1 quart of lukewarm water. This method applies also to rattan decorative articles and furniture. The wetting and drying occasioned by the cleaning process will help tighten sagging or stretched cane seats, which are prone to breaking.

WICKERWARE: Bamboo and reed porch furniture are best maintained when given a coat of varnish—or enamel if a color is desired—before each season, applied from an aerosol spray, for clean appearance and protection from moisture. Routine dusting or vacuuming will suffice, except that sticky substances on chair arms and scuffings of furniture legs require washing with a wall-type detergent (Spic and Span, Mr. Clean, Fantastik) and hot water, scrubbing with a nylon-mesh pad as needed.

RATTAN AND WICKER FURNITURE, REPAIR: A frequent problem is loss of the reed bindings on arms and back, which results when the rattan strips break and unwind. Remove all loose binding, replace with a new wicker strip (available from hobby houses or mail-order firms). Soak the rattan in warm water until pliable. Brush wood glue on the surfaces to be repaired, securing the new end with a brad until the glue sets. Wrap the wicker around the glue-coated arm, then tack down the other end. The strip will adhere and become part of the chair. Varnishing will help match it to the original surface.

RECLINER CHAIR: Vinyl upholstery needs only sponging with a mild detergent and water, then waxing to preserve flexibility of the plastic. The headrest requires frequent cleaning because the alcohol in hair oils and conditioners dries the vinyl and causes it to crack. Clean with Fantastik spray, rinse and dry. Do not use mineral solvents on the plastic.

Textile upholstery is cleaned according to the specifications for the particular fibers. Separating zippered covers from their cushions for cleaning is not recommended because of shrinking in the cleaning process. (See *Upholstery,* page 175.)

SURFACE REPAIRS: A shallow dent or gouge in wood sometimes can be "lifted" by steaming or soaking; minor scratches may be blended in with pigmented wax or plastic varnish. Deeper gouges and scratches can be corrected by the old-time "burning in" method with melted stick shellac, which requires a deft touch. Details follow:

1. *Stick Shellac Patching:* Remove any wax or polish with a turpentine-moistened pad, scrape and sand to remove the old finish around the blemish. Wipe off dust. Touch up the bare wood with color stain.

Select a shellac to match the original finish. Light an alcohol lamp and heat your spatula. Touch the shellac to the spatula so that a little melts onto the blade, pass the blade again over the flame (tilting the blade to concentrate the molten shellac at one edge), then immediately turn the blade and draw it quickly across the scratch. Examine the result; add a bit more if needed. The objective is to fill the scratch just flush with the surface.

The next step is rubbing the patch with dampened rottenstone or fine pumice to remove surface irregularities and to feather the edges into the surrounding surface. Blending is done with a powder stain moistened with lacquer-thinner and applied with an artist's brush, then rubbed with a felt pad to a high luster.

2. *Steaming:* Use a cotton swab dipped in turpentine to dissolve surface wax at the dent. Place a blotter over the area, moisten with a few drops of water, then press down with a steam iron. One or two short bursts of steam should suffice, but don't overdo the steaming, as it may affect the rest of the finish.

Deeper gouges are packed with wood-filler or spackle plaster after cutting away the compressed fibers with knife or chisel. Leave sufficient depth for application of shellac in matching color.

INK STAINS: If the finish is worn, the stain will penetrate deeply and be impossible to remove. Minimize stain by bleaching with household ammonia or a strong solution of oxalic acid (poisonous). If on surface only, rub in mixture of rottenstone and light oil, made into a paste. (See *Stains: Ink,* page 163.)

ALCOHOL SPOTS AND RINGS: These white rings are usually caused by glasses containing alcoholic beverages. Dampen a cloth with spirits of camphor and dab on the spot, let it dry about 30 minutes and then rub down with rottenstone mixed with a light oil (mineral oil, salad oil or 3-in-1 oil). Table salt mixed with a light oil is also said to be effective. Another method is to apply a thick paste of grade FFF (very fine) pumice and oil, rubbed until the spot is removed. Toothpaste plus baking soda also may eliminate white rings.

Garage Floors: Rare is the car that doesn't drip a bit of oil or grease now and then, creating nasty stained areas in the garage and driveway. A shallow metal pan left on the garage floor under the motor section will protect the paving; a cardboard carton, cut down for clearance, also can do the job and can be discarded periodically.

An old rubber inner tube, sliced open and tacked along the edge of the garage door, seals the door bottom to prevent dirt and leaves being blown into the garage.

Cleanup of a garage floor is best done with sawdust and a grease solvent, allowed to soak in for an hour or so to absorb the grease, then swept away. It may be necessary to scrub the garage floor or concrete driveway with a stiff-bristled brush and mineral spirits (turps, varnolene). Repeat the process until all the soaked-in oil is removed. A solution of laundry detergent with 1 cup of chlorine bleach can eliminate any stains; use this method on brick or concrete driveways, but not on asphalt, which can become softened.

Garbage Cans: After flushing cans with a garden hose, sanitize them by pouring in a solution of washing soda or ammonia. Keep covers in good condition so they fit tightly.

Garbage Grinder: An electric undersink waste disposer provides a welcome relief from garbage handling and is an important step in sanitation. Constantly improved, these appliances now handle large bones and stringy vegetables that formerly caused jamming or overloading. Do not grind metal, glass or paper, or permit cutlery to fall into the opening.

Continuous-feed grinders have become the more popular of two types. The device is controlled by a wall switch and can be turned on whenever desired. In the batch-feed type, waste is accumulated in the container, and the machine can be started only by placing a cover over the sink drain opening. With both types, it is important to keep the cold water running while the motor is on.

Jamming of the grinder blades may occur with either type. If the overload switch has been tripped, just press the red reset button at the bottom of the machine. Jammed cutters can be released by working back and forth with a hexagonal wrench fitted into a recess at the bottom, while some models permit reversing the motor to clear the blockage.

Ice cubes and citrus fruit rinds placed into the grinder will counteract unpleasant odors. Never put caustic drain cleaners (lye) into the disposal.

Gardening Tools: Keep a pail of sand handy in the garage or potting shed; mix a pint or so of lowest-cost motor oil into the sand. After using the spade, claw digger or other tool, scrape off the soil with a broad putty knife and plunge the tool into the sand pail. That will at one time scour the tool so it is perfectly clean and also coat it with oil sufficiently to prevent rust. Store the tools on wall hooks in a dry place such as the garage.

Gasoline: The odor of gasoline splattered on the hands while filling the car tank or a lawn mower can persist even after thorough washing. A little shaving lotion or toilet water rubbed on the hands will mask the odor, as will lemon rind. Add bleach to the wash water when laundering clothing that has been affected by a gasoline spill. A clear odor of gasoline may indicate a leak—from a fuel line connection at the carburator or at the gasoline tank itself—and warrants a thorough checkup.

Glassware

BOTTLES: A narrow round brush such as that used for nursery bottles simplifies the removal from bottles of any foreign matter. Half fill with detergent solution, shake vigorously. Jars and bottles that have been standing for an extended period can be deodorized by rinsing with a solution of mustard in water or of diluted chlorine bleach. Steep some tea in warm water to wash glasses, jars and vases—watch them regain their sparkle instantly.

CRYSTAL: Wash unornamented crystalware in an ammonia solution, 2 tablespoons to 1 quart of water (or proportionate), which will dissolve any filmy residue. Rinse thoroughly and polish with a soft cloth. Do not use ammonia on ornamented glassware, however, as it may fade the decorative trim. An aerosol-type crystal cleaner, Sparkle Safe, safely produces a brilliant shine on glassware, requires no drying, won't leave spots.

GLASS COOKWARE: See *Cookware: Pyrex,* page 61.

STEMWARE: Avoid damaging delicate glassware when placing it in hot water by slipping the glass in edgewise and holding onto it until the glass reaches bottom. Never plunge icy glassware into very hot water, or conversely, hot glasses into icy water.

Wash stemware with mild detergent, lifting the glass by its stem one piece at a time and dipping it into the solution. Place on paper or soft towels to drain; polish with soft towel to prevent water spots.

VASES: Narrow-necked glass vases can be scrubbed clean on the inside without a brush. Pour in half a cup of raw rice (the uncooked or converted type), fill the vase halfway with warm water, and add a dash of dish detergent and 1 tablespoon of chlorine bleach. Cover the mouth of the vase with the palm of one hand and shake vigorously. When clean, pour out the contents and rinse well.

Inside stains can be removed by filling the vase with warm water and some tea leaves. Allow to stand for several hours, then wash with soap suds and rinse. Another effective method is to soak the vase in a pot with heated vinegar.

Gluing: Modern adhesives enable you to successfully repair a broken plate or porcelain figurine, replace a cup handle, reset the stones in costume jewelry, and reattach loosened furniture veneers (see chart below). The result is usually a waterproof, shock-resistant repair that withstands both dishwasher and freezer temperatures.

Use these adhesives for reattaching metal or plastic moldings on your car, repairing tears in rubber boots, cementing house numbers to brick or stone walls, repairing tennis racket handles and other sports equipment.

Most cements come in tubes with nozzle caps that preserve the cement for further use. Silicones and epoxies will bond almost anything—metals, glass, ceramic tile, rubber, wood, stone and certain plastics. For example, silicone adhesive will bond the glass sides of an aquarium, the joints remaining sealed against leaks for 10 years and longer. (Brands of silicone adhesives include Weldwood, Devcon, Dow Corning, Magic American.)

Acetate-base cements are excellent for nonporous articles like porcelains. (The most famous brand is Duco by DuPont.) Some pressure on the repair joint is required; use rubber bands, properly placed and reinforced with masking tape.

The electric glue gun is a small, inexpensive appliance that heats a white cartridge in just minutes. Squeezing the trigger emits a thin bead of adhesive of which a spot is applied. The parts are then pressed firmly together for a few seconds until the glue cools and hardens. The resultant joint will be extremely strong. Make certain the parts fit together neatly before gluing.

Epoxy cements come in two parts: the resin and hardener, which are mixed in exactly equal portions. Epoxy cements will bond almost anything to anything, produce the strongest joints, even attach a sheet metal patch to seal an auto exhaust muffler. Use the cement immediately after mixing the ingredients. Epoxy application is greatly simplified by Loctite's disposable two-section plastic cup that contains the correct amount of each part, enough to do a single cementing job. Just penetrate the cover, mix with a wooden spatula, and apply. Squeeze the parts together for a minute or so until the adhesive sets; apply weights or wrap tightly with adhesive tape for at least 8 hours, until the bonding is fully accomplished.

Instant-setting glues will do almost any kind of bonding. A two-part type, Minute Bond Adhesive, has a primer coat that is sprayed on both parts, then adhesive is applied from a tube, and the parts are pressed together for about a minute. The adhesive attains 60 percent of its strength in just a few minutes, full strength in 24 hours.

A more recently developed type called "instant" adhesive is available in many well known brands (such as Krazy Glue, and Super Glue). One drop forms a bond with sheer strength equal to a ton of weight. Apply it directly from the tube, or with a wooden spatula; press the parts together just for a moment. Extreme caution is necessary with "instant" glue— if any gets on your fingers it can instantly glue them together. If this happens, apply acetone (nail polish remover) immediately to peel them apart, or call a doctor or rush to the emergency room of the nearest hospital. Be careful to avoid contact with the eyes.

GLUES

Types	Uses	Characteristics
White Glue (Polyvinyl Resin)	Closely fitted wood joints, cloth, paper, porous materials.	Sets in 1 to 2 hours at room temperature. Requires clamping. Comes in paste form, ready to use. Not waterproof.

GLUES

Types	Uses	Characteristics
Casein Glue	Furniture joints, exterior surfaces.	Comes in powder form, for mixing with water.
Contact Cement	Laminates, Formica, plastic, wall panels, wall tiles, porous articles, kitchen countertops.	Made of dissolved latex. Bonds instantly on contact. Comes in flammable and nonflammable types. Needs no clamping. Ready to use.
Epoxy	Repair of ceramics and metals, joining metal to rubber or glass. As additive with cement, permits the thin-layer resurfacing of concrete, and pointing of brickwork.	Two-part mixture, sets and dries in less than half an hour, reaches full strength in 8 hours. Needs pressure.
Hide Glue	Restoring antique furniture, general wood repairs.	Applied hot or cold, depending on type; needs clamping, overnight setting. Strong but not waterproof.
Clear Plastic Cement, Styrene, Vinyl	General repairs on wood, ceramics, jewelry. Also styrene glue for rigid plastics. Vinyl glue for flexible plastics.	Work can be held together until glue sets in 15 to 20 seconds. Beware of fingers becoming fixed by glue. Flammable.
Resorcinol Glue	Waterproof, used for exterior outdoor furniture, plywood, boat hulls.	Comes in two parts, one a liquid resin, the other a powdered catalyst. Needs pressure clamping for 12 hours.
Metal Glues	These are fillers rather than glues, as they have only slight holding power.Filling auto body dents, smooth gouges in metal objects.	Apply with putty knife; sets quickly on exposure.
Instant Glues	Bond almost anything— joint need not be precisely fitted.	Holds almost on instant contact. Caution: Do not get glue on fingers. Need only momentary squeeze pressure.

GLUES		
Types	Uses	Characteristics
Electric Gun Glues	Bond odd-shaped parts with caulk-type heated glue.	One-inch glue cartridge heated by electricity; glue is squeezed out by trigger pressure. Needs no clamping.

"Gold Filled" Articles: Gold filling is similar to "gold plating" except that a very thin layer of gold is attached to the base metal, usually brass, by mechanical rather than chemical or electrolytic means. Wiping with a dampened chamois or soft cloth usually is sufficient to remove surface dirt, but if the object is coated with grime or stubborn soil, use a silver or metal polish lightly, so as not to rub through the surface metal. Keep salt and perspiration away from gold-filled articles; always wipe dry after washing.

Gold Leaf: Restore luster by rubbing lightly with absorbent cotton or a cellulose sponge, moistened with turpentine or vinegar, a process called burnishing. Another method of cutting surface grime is wiping with a cloth dampened with a solution of equal parts alcohol and ammonia, then polishing with lemon oil. Gold leaf will have maximum brilliance if left in its natural state, but if it is subject to frequent handling or hard wear, apply a thin coating of fresh white shellac, diluted half and half with alcohol. Picture frames, statuary and decorative gold borders around a desk top, may require the protective shellac coating.

Golf Balls: Your drives will go yards farther with superclean golf balls, says the manufacturer of a cleaning solvent called On the Ball, a claim that has been difficult to confirm. Another cleaner for the same purpose has a circular sponge in a container with a hole at the center through which the ball is rotated for washing after the sponge is moistened with water.

Gutters. See *Roof Gutters,* page 142.

Hair Brushes: Both nylon and natural-fiber bristles can be cleaned by soaking in soap and water to which a teaspoon of ammonia is added to cut the grease. Use a fine comb to clear the bristles of entangled hair. Rinse, stand on the bristles to drain. When dry, turn the brush over.

Brushes that are made entirely of nylon, including the handle, can be sterilized in boiling water. This cannot be done if the handle is of acrylic plastic, which becomes softened under heat, or of wood, which should not be soaked with water.

Electric hair brushes such as the Snoopy Lectric Comb and Brush, can be washed safely only if they are battery powered. Do not immerse other electrical brushes in water.

Head Lice: When an epidemic of head lice sweeps a community, it is advisable to check your children regularly in order to spot any infestation in its early stages. The bugs are spread by clothing and towels in addition to direct contact; personal cleanliness in itself offers no protection. The eggs, called nits, are easy to find if you part the hair every inch or so; they resemble dandruff but are firmly attached to the hair, usually very close to the scalp. The bugs may escape detection until they become quite numerous.

If nits or lice are discovered, shampoo the hair with a disinfecting shampoo formulated for the purpose. Most contain lindane (gamma benzene hexachloride). Work up a lather with the shampoo, allow to remain at least 4 minutes, then rinse. Be careful to avoid contact with the eyes. All the bugs are killed at once by the shampoo, but not necessarily all of the nits, and a second application a week later may be necessary. Comb out the nits using a fine comb dipped repeatedly in hot vinegar. It is advisable to cut off any hairs that still have nits, disposing of the hairs carefully.

Check all other family members for several days. A thorough housecleaning also is essential. Wash combs and brushes in hot vinegar. Launder all clothing, sheets, towels, dolls and anything else that may have become contaminated. Use chlorine bleach in the laundering where possible. Articles that cannot be readily washed may be stored in a sealed plastic bag for a month or so, after which time they may be considered free of the infestation because the parasite lice hatch after 6 days and cannot survive away from a host.

Hand Cleaners: Oatmeal is an exceptionally gentle but efficient hand cleaner, capable of removing grease and oil and grime; it also reduces or eliminates odors from kerosene or gasoline. Just pick up a small quantity of oatmeal flakes, moisten slightly with water or milk, and rub. You can even let the used oatmeal go down the drain, but not all in one clump.

Roughened hands benefit from rubbing with the pulp of lemon or grapefruit rinds. A mild hand cleaner can be made by joining cornmeal, borax and sodium perborate (oxygen bleach.) For more powerful action, combine trisodium phosphate (TSP) or fine pumice powder with glycerine or a petroleum jelly like Vaseline.

Hand cleaners that have been around a long time and have been found satisfactory are Lava Soap and Gresolvent, in powder and paste form.

There are many waterless cleaners. One of the oldest and best known is DuPont's Pro-Tek, a creamy white paste, applied to the hands before starting work. It adheres to the skin to act as a protective coating. It is easily washed away with soap and water, removing tar, ink, grease, coal dust and similar surface soil. This type of cleaner is especially useful where water is not available for washup.

House Siding

WOODEN SIDING: Dingy or grimy clapboards do not necessarily indicate that the time has come for repainting—a good scrubbing often will provide a fresh clean look. Use a scrub brush, the garden hose, and a detergent solution. Stubborn spots may require full-strength cleaners like Soilax, TSP90,

Spic and Span. A circular brush on a long stick or metal tubing—the kind used for car washing—will reach some of the higher parts of the wall, but a two-story house with a high peak may require use of an extension ladder.

Scrub and rinse from the bottom up, to avoid streaking by runoff of dirty water as you work higher. At each section, first hose down to remove surface dirt, scrub where needed, then rinse thoroughly with the hose. A spray attachment on the hose will step up the pressure for better rinsing.

Premature repainting, in addition to the considerable needless expense, also can be harmful in piling extra paint onto existing coats that have not yet become sufficiently weathered to reduce their bulk and weight. There may indeed be small sections where the paint has actually deteriorated, for which the best treatment is touching up with matching paint after sanding or burning off the remaining old paint with a propane torch.

ALUMINUM SIDING: The rains effectively clean aluminum house walls, although dirt may accumulate under the eaves or roof overhang. If very soiled or discolored, scrub those sections with a strong detergent, reaching with a brush on a long pole or climbing a ladder. Rinse with a sponge. Spraying with the garden hose upward from the ground is questionable, as water will enter vent slots on the underside of the siding panels.

FIELDSTONE SIDING: Rust stains sometimes develop from iron fittings in the fieldstone walls. These stains may yield to rust-remover chemicals, at least partially, in which case the variegated coloring of the stone may mask the residual rust. If the rust has not penetrated deeply, as is likely, the best approach would be to chip off part of the facing with a sharp chisel, thus obtaining for a while at least a fresh new surface. When painting the house trim be very careful not to splatter the fieldstone, as the paint spots will be most difficult to remove.

Humidity in the Home: Where there is too little moisture in the air, usually in cold weather, respiratory discomfort results, furniture joints come apart, and static electricity causes unpleasant shocks at doorknobs. But if there is excessive water vapor in the air (a high relative humidity) it condenses on pipes, windows and walls, drips all over the place, and creates dampness that fosters mildew.

Warm air holds more moisture than cool air—that is one key to understanding relative humidity; expressed as a percentage, a relative humidity figure represents not the actual quantity of moisture but rather the ratio of water vapor in the air to the total amount of water vapor the air could hold at a given temperature. An air conditioner or a dehumidifier lowers the relative humidity in a room. While a 50 percent reading is considered normal, most persons find a range from 30 to 40 percent most comfortable in hot weather, 50 to 60 percent in cold weather.

There is a constant interchange of air between inside and outside the home, through the walls as well as through open windows and other unsealed entryways. Cool air in the home draws a lower proportion of water vapor, so intermittent functioning of the air conditioner helps keep vapor level low, drawing moisture out of the air, expelling it outside. The humidistat is thus an important instrument in the prevention of mildew, activating the air conditioner to prevent excess dampness that would result from higher temperatures.

Stagnant warm and humid air in an attic that lacks adequate ventilation may cause rotting of structural timber in addition to extensive mildewing. A louvered vent at each end wall, near the peak, to allow release of moist air, is necessary. These vents must provide at least 1 square foot of opening for every 300 square feet of attic floor area. Mildew spotting of the rafters can be washed off with a solution of 1 quart chlorine bleach to 3 quarts of water. (See *Mildew,* page 112.)

Ice Skates: Wipe blades dry after each use; put on blade guards before storing. The shoes can be kept supple by daubing with saddle soap, which contains lanolin.

Ink Stains: See *Furniture,* page 81, and *Stains: Ink,* page 163.

Insulation: Increasing the insulation in an existing house for better heating economy is difficult and does not always achieve the desired result. Insulation can be added in the form of blankets, batts or granules, between the attic floor joists or above the ceiling if the attic has an enclosed room. In this procedure, the original insulation batts, if there are any between the floor joists, sometimes are cut away and allowed to drop down to allow space for thicker blankets, but this alters the vapor barrier, which should face the inside surface. The old batts thus may become soaked with moisture from vapor penetration. It's better to discard the old insulation material if it is inadequate, replace it with blankets having a heat resistance rating of at least R-22 (6½ inch thickness), which is adequate for the average home in most sections of the country. Some parts of the attic extend far into the eaves and cannot be reached because of insufficient overhead clearance; thus they will remain poorly insulated and cause continued heat loss.

Another method is blowing insulation fibers into side walls from the outside through holes drilled in the siding or openings made by removing a number of bricks in the walls. This procedure, done by commercial firms having the required equipment, has shortcomings because firestops in the walls prevent complete distribution of the fibers.

Better-fitting windows, properly weather-sealed doors and closed fireplace dampers will do much to lessen heat loss in existing homes. Newly constructed homes, on the contrary, are planned for adequate insulation.

Kitchen Exhaust Fan: Much as an exhaust fan contributes to your comfort by eliminating hot fumes and cooking odors, it serves almost as importantly in protecting the walls and ceiling from a greasy coating and discoloration of the paint. An effective fan is one with a strong enough motor to move the required amount of air to accomplish those purposes. Some fans are all noise, no action, because they are not vented to the exterior. Exhaust fans are most effective when the motor section is located on the outside wall, helping keep sound to a minimum. This is accomplished in the Nutone exterior mounted models by having the blades designed to pull the air out through the wall rather than pushing the air forward from the inside. The more powerful exterior motor thus does a better job with almost silent operation.

The exhaust fan has filters that trap grease to prevent its accumulation in the duct. The filter is easy to remove and it's advisable to make a weekly routine of washing it by soaking it in a pan with a wall detergent for a few minutes. When removing the filter, make it a practice to wipe the duct with a soapy sponge to remove any grease.

Charcoal filters have a limited air-cleaning value and require occasional replacement.

Knives

ELECTRIC KNIFE: Release the two serrated blades from the handle for washing (after disconnecting the electric cord) by pressing the red button on the handle. Separate the blades by disengaging the one with the rivet from the keyhole slot in the other blade. Clean the blades in hot soapy water; wipe with a folded-over sponge, rinse and dry. Store in plastic blade pocket. These serrated blades cannot be sharpened; replace dull blades with new ones.

KNIFE SAFETY: Plug the cord into the knife before connecting it to a wall receptacle. Keep the electric cord away from the cutting area and hot surfaces that can damage the insulation; do not cut frozen foods or bones. Carve foods on a plastic or wooden cutting board whenever possible, never on china or metal surfaces. Pull wall plug before disengaging the cord from the knife body. Never immerse the knife body in water.

A cordless knife is the safest kind, as there is no cord to get in the way and the knife can be used outdoors, right at the barbecue. The knife is powered by a battery, which can be recharged by plugging into any house receptacle. Above all, keep fingers away from the cutting edge of an electric knife —even when it's not in use.

KITCHEN KNIVES: Store knives of various sizes in a wall rack with individual slots so the sharp edges do not come in contact with other hard surfaces. Do all slicing on a wooden or plastic board. Cutting food on a glazed plate or metal pan dulls the blade. Wash knives with a folded sponge and dry to retain brightness. Don't put knives in the dishwasher unless this is specified as safe by the manufacturer. Sharp knives are safer to use because they do not require the pressure or force that must be applied to dull blades. (See *Sharpening,* page 150.)

Labels

CLOTHING: Damage to garments from improper cleaning and laundering has no doubt been greatly reduced by implementation of federal regulations requiring labels on garments, and on textiles intended for sewing into garments, clearly specifying the laundering, drying, ironing, dry cleaning and other procedures required to properly maintain or care for the garment, including cautions against methods that would be detrimental.

How to interpret the labels? Use the accompanying chart

as a guide. Anything that is shown as "washable" can be either laundered or dry-cleaned. But some say DO NOT DRY CLEAN, others say DRY CLEAN, BUT NOT WITH A PETROLEUM PRODUCT, and others may state DRY CLEAN ONLY. Do not assume anything that is not specifically stated.

APPAREL LABELS AND THEIR MEANING

When Label Reads:	It Means:
MACHINE WASHABLE	
Machine wash	Wash, bleach, dry and press by any customary method including commercial laundering and dry cleaning
Home launder only	Same as above but do not use commercial laundering
No chlorine bleach	Do not use chlorine bleach; oxygen bleach may be used
No bleach	Do not use any type of bleach
Cold wash Cold rinse	Use cold water from tap or cold washing machine setting
Warm wash Warm rinse	Use warm water or warm washing machine setting
Hot wash	Use hot water or hot washing machine setting
No spin	Remove wash load before final machine spin cycle
Delicate cycle Gentle cycle	Use appropriate machine setting; otherwise wash by hand
Durable press cycle Permanent press cycle	Use appropriate machine setting; otherwise use warm wash, cold rinse and short spin cycle
Wash separately	Wash alone or with like colors
NON-MACHINE WASHING	
Hand wash	Launder only by hand in lukewarm (hand comfortable) water. May be bleached. May be dry-cleaned

APPAREL LABELS AND THEIR MEANING

When Label Reads:	It Means:
Hand wash only	Same as above, but do not dry-clean
Hand wash separately	Hand wash alone or with like colors
No bleach	Do not use bleach
Damp wipe	Clean surface with damp cloth or sponge

HOME DRYING

Tumble dry	Dry in tumble dryer at specified setting—high, medium, low or no heat
Tumble dry Remove promptly	Same as above, but in absence of cool-down cycle remove at once when tumbling stops
Drip dry	Hang wet and allow to dry with hand shaping only
Line dry	Hang damp and allow to dry
No wring No twist	Hang dry, drip dry or dry flat only. Handle carefully to prevent wrinkles and distortion
Dry flat	Lay garment on flat surface
Block to dry	Maintain original size and shape while drying

IRONING OR PRESSING

Cool iron	Set iron at lowest setting
Warm iron	Set iron at medium setting
Hot iron	Set iron at hot setting
Do not iron	Do not iron or press with heat
Steam iron	Iron or press with steam
Iron damp	Dampen garment before ironing

MISCELLANEOUS

Dry-clean only	Garment should be dry-cleaned only, including self-service
Professionally dry-clean only	Do not use self-service dry-cleaning
No dry-clean	Use recommended care instructions. No dry-cleaning materials to be used.

Note: Exempt from labeling requirements are furs and leather goods, sheer hosiery (but care labels must be on the package), disposable items and those that do not need any maintenance, such as see-through garments.

FLAMMABILITY: Label instructions for the care of flame-resistant garments, draperies and other textiles should be followed carefully. A typical label may be worded "Launder with phosphate detergent; do not use soap." The reason is that the reaction of soap with hard-water minerals can diminish the flame resistance built into the fabric, while the phosphates increase alkalinity. Some communities, however, have banned the sale of phosphate-containing detergents because they promote excessive algae growth (eutrophication) that chokes lakes and streams. This restriction presents only a minor difficulty in homes whose water is soft, but in hard-water areas it is advisable to check with the local water company for advice on available phosphate substitutes to preserve the flame-proof quality.

INSECTICIDES: Labels on insecticide containers show the ingredients, the kinds of insects for which the product will be effective, the safe methods of application, warnings on toxicity or flammability and instructions for first aid in the event of poisoning or injury. (See also *Pest Control,* page 125.)

REMOVING LABELS AND STICKERS: Bottle and jar labels can be removed by soaking in water for 15 minutes or so. Hot water gives a faster result. Place jar in the sink with enough water to cover until label can be rubbed off. Stickers on auto windshields usually must be scraped off with a razor blade. Pressure-sensitive (self-adhesive) labels have a rubber cement coating on the back and usually just peel off when a corner is loosened. A residue of rubber cement that may remain can be rubbed off or removed with cleaning fluid or acetone. (See *Rubber Cement,* page 143 and *Automobiles: License Stickers,* page 33.)

Lampshades: Plastic shades that have washable ornamentation are laundered most easily by dunking into soapy water in the bathtub. You can do several small shades at the same time. Rinse in clear water and let stand to air-dry; but wipe metal parts carefully. Fabric shades and those with gilt designs or textile borders can be cleaned with an ionic spray (Shade Safe). The spray cleans fabric and paper shades safely without shrinkage or stretching, leaving a thin film that repels soiling and inhibits corrosion of the shade frame.

A different dry cleaning method (Rubgum) employs a sort of soft powder puff containing a very fine powder that sifts through the cloth cover onto the shade. Light rubbing restores the original luster of the shade material, although this may be difficult on ruffled and similar shades.

Lucite shades are simply wiped clean with a damp cloth. As the plastic is subject to scratching, do not use any abrasive cleaner or coarse scrubbing pad.

Lawn Umbrellas: After a season or two of weathering, lawn umbrellas, deck-chair panels and canopies tend to look drab, colors faded. Dry-clean with Rubgum powder sack, or rejuvenate with special canvas paint. Apply one to three coats in straight, uniform strokes, allowing overnight drying between coats; finish with a coat of varnish if a glossy surface is desired.

Keep lawn umbrellas, awnings and other canvas equipment open after a rain until completely dry, to protect against mildew. Store out of season in a cool, dry and airy place, properly folded.

Leather: Even in the thinnest cross-section to which it is sliced —for gloves, billfolds, desk covers and the like—leather is very durable, will last for decades with proper care. But when it loses its oil, leather becomes brittle and tends to crack.

A good leather-conditioner is saddle soap, containing lanolin derived from sheep's wool. Also effective are neat's-foot oil, castor oil and cod-liver oil. Rub in the oil with the fingers, allow the excess to soak in for an hour or so, then wipe the surface to prevent pickup of grit. Saddle soap also serves as a cleaning agent.

Always allow wet leather to dry slowly in the open air. Drape garments to their normal shape on hangers away from direct heat. Boots, shoes and luggage must not be left to dry on the floor in a closet. Remember that leather is most susceptible to mildew when it is wet or damp. Keep these articles out in the open, in a lighted place, until dry. (See also *Mildew*, page 112 and *Suede*, page 171.)

OILED WORK SHOES: The combination of waterproofing and softness can be retained by cleaning only with a mild soap and water, followed when dry with an application of sulfonated castor oil, neat's-foot oil or cod-liver oil. The frequency of oiling is determined by the degree of flexibility and waterproofing desired.

SMOOTH AND POLISHED LEATHER: Wipe off surface dirt with a damp cloth. If only slightly soiled, an application of polish and wax will restore the finish. Very soiled leather is best washed with a neutral soap (any good grade of toilet or castile soap will do) or specially compounded saddle soap (Goddard Saddlers Wax) containing lanolin. Patent leather belts, handbags, chair coverings, briefcases and luggage should be treated with castor-oil or neat's-foot oil; use a thin coat of petroleum jelly (Vaseline) on bookbindings. A good silicone polish on garments prevents rain-spotting. Stains or spots that are not removed by soap and water may sometimes be lifted with a suitable solvent or with a cloth moistened with methylated spirit, depending on the type of stain. However, all solvents must be used with discretion to avoid leaving ring marks or altering the original color.

TABLETOPS: When the leather cover on a table, desk or jewelry box begins to curl up at the corners, reglue it promptly before the leather shrinks and will need to be stretched to fit —a difficult task when combined with gluing.

Coat both surfaces, that is, the exposed wood top and the underside of the leather, with rubber cement. Keep the parts separated with a toothpick or similar spacer, while the cement sets for about 20 minutes; then roll the leather down into the corner. Start from the bonded part of the leather, move the fingers forward to the corner while pressing down the leather, a method that will avoid trapping air bubbles under the leather. Finally, tap down hard on the cemented leather to be sure of a good bond.

UPHOLSTERY LEATHER: Routine vacuuming of dust and occasional cleaning with a damp cloth, followed by an application of saddle soap or other oil-based conditioner, should keep upholstery leather in good condition indefinitely. Keep wetting to a minimum. Little can be done to rejuvenate leather surfaces that have been scuffed or ripped, replacement being about the only practical course. Large leather sections can be obtained from crafts supply firms for do-it-yourself applications.

WHITE LEATHER: Smooth calfskin, kid gloves and shoes are washed with a damp, sudsy cloth. Avoid excessive wetting and wipe at once with a clean dry cloth; then apply a high-quality white commercial cleaner (Lanol White, SnoShoo) that restores the attractive finish and replaces the oils lost through wear and washing.

Lighting

LIGHT BULBS: Wipe bulbs occasionally with a dry dustcloth for cleanliness and better illumination. Remove a burned-out bulb by turning it counter-clockwise, slowly and steadily, so the glass bulb does not twist loose of its base. Always replace bulb at once; it's best not to leave the socket empty, even for a short while, so have the replacement at hand.

APPLIANCE BULBS: Replace existing appliance bulbs only with the special type designed to withstand the extremes of heat and cold in the oven or refrigerator. These appliance bulbs can be purchased at supermarkets and hardware stores.

The small tubular lamps in the control panels of washing machines, dryers and ovens can be purchased at appliance-parts stores. Use the size and type recommended in your appliance instruction booklet. Many clothes dryers also have an ultraviolet lamp, which eventually burns out but is difficult to replace because it can be reached only from the rear of the dryer drum, which requires removing the back panel of the dryer for access.

FLUORESCENT LAMPS: Wipe the lamp tubes and fixture reflectors or light diffusion covers with a dustcloth monthly, being careful not to twist the tube in its socket, which might cause it to loosen and fall out. Lamps that flicker on and off, or have dark rings at the ends, need to be replaced; it's wasteful of energy to wait until the lamps burn out. Hold the lamp at both ends, make about a quarter-turn, and the lamp pins will slip out of the retainer clips at each end. Be careful not to drop the tube —it will shatter into thousands of fragments that are difficult to sweep up.

Fluorescent fixtures come usually in 15-, 20-, 30-, 40- and 100-watt sizes. The 20-watt tube is 2 feet long, the 40-watt is 4 feet long. There are several shades of light—daylight, cold light, blue white, etc.—including the pink lamps used for house plants.

You may find replacing the lamps is somewhat trouble-some at first. The tube has two connector pins at each end, intended to snap into spring-loaded retainer receptacles. Hold the lamp so that the pins are lined up vertically—that is, one above the other. Slip the pins at one end of the lamp straight up into the receptacle, then push the pins at the other end into place.

Make a quarter-turn of the lamp either way. Don't let go of the lamp until you feel the click and have checked to be certain that *both* ends are securely held. After several tries you won't find lamp installation so difficult; just remember, if only one end is locked in, the lamp will slip out and fall.

Luminous kitchen ceilings collect dust, cooking grease and trapped insects, so need to be cleaned regularly. Remove the translucent plastic panels by lifting them off the metal hanger channels, grasping each panel securely and letting it down carefully so it doesn't drop and become damaged. Wash the panels individually in the sink or laundry tub with a detergent solution; wipe dry before replacing. Most of the panels are of the same dimensions, so there's no problem identifying them for replacement positions.

Lightning: City dwellers are not generally subject to the haz-ards of lighting bolts because they are protected by concen-trations of tall buildings and other structures that draw the lightning and direct it harmlessly to the ground. Underwriters Laboratories (UL) recommends certain precautions for persons living in open areas, or when they are in certain situations.

If you're out of doors when a thunderstorm starts, head for a substantial building, preferably one with a grounded frame. (Of course you wouldn't be able to identify such a building, but that's what you need.) Places to avoid are golf courses, open hilltops, tall isolated trees. Stay clear also of telephone poles, power lines, wire fences or other structures that could serve as conductors of electricity. When at the beach, stay out of the water, avoid open boats, get to proper shelter as quickly as you can.

An automobile offers excellent protection against lightning; stay in the car throughout the storm. Park if you can, but not alongside power lines or under a trestle, and avoid touching the car's body metal.

At home, avoid contact with plumbing and heating lines. It's best not to turn on the television or other electric appliance during an electric storm, although a proper UL-approved lightning arrester on the antenna system will discharge any lightning bolt harmlessly. A sudden surge of electrical current, however, may damage the TV set.

Linoleum: See *Floors: Linoleum,* page 77.

Lubrication: A handy oilcan, used judiciously in the right places, can make things go smoother around the home, eliminate squeaks from both new shoes and old hinges, prevent appliance breakdowns and save considerable money by making equipment last longer.

Sealed bearings in many motors, appliances and tools have indeed reduced the need for lubrication. Many home articles and installations, however, still need to be greased for proper functioning. It's important, however, to know where and what kind of lubrication to use in each instance, and just as important, how much. Sometimes degreasing—dissolving and wiping away the grease when there's too much—ends the trouble.

An attic fan motor—the belt-drive type—has oil cups on the shaft bearing at each end. Just one or two drops of #30

motor oil at the start of each season does the trick—the motor
can run continually for days on end, with just that much oil.
Any greater amount might seep onto the commutator and
cause the motor to fail. The fan bearings also must be lu-
bricated—usually only once each season—with a few drops of
light oil in the oil cup at each end of the fan shaft.

New lubricants in spray cans (WD-40, Slide-All, Handycan,
many others) are convenient to use and more effective than
old-type oilcans for certain conditions. Squirt the oil directly
onto the squeaky mechanisms.

Lock cylinders at home and in the car can become difficult
to open, but don't go shooting gobs of oil into the keyways
because that will cause grime to freeze the cylinder pins. The
right lubricant here is graphite powder, puffed into the key-
way from the graphite container.

Many manufacturers recommend specific lubricants for
tools and other products. Refer to the instruction booklets or
tags on the equipment.

The chart below lists items around the home that need
lubrication. The type of lubricant mentioned is only a general, not a specific recommendation.

LUBRICATION GUIDE

Attic fan bearings	#30 motor oil
Auto (various parts)	refer to owner's manual
Baby carriage (wheel bearings)	Vaseline
Bench grinder bearings	light oil
Bicycle (wheel bearings, yoke)	light oil
Cabinet door hinges	light oil
Casement windows (rotors, hinges)	light grease, Vaseline
Door hinges (pull hinge pins)	Vaseline
Door lock cylinders	graphite
Door spring latch	silicone lubricant
Drawer runners	silicone wax

Drill press quill	stick wax
Furniture casters (ball bearings)	light oil
Garage door hardware	silicone oil
Golf cart wheels	light grease
Grandfather clock	very light oil—lightly
Lawn mower	light grease
Patio door track	silicone
Portable tools—sabre saw	special lube
Power saw bearings	#30 motor oil
Record changer	special formula
Sewing machine	3-in-1 oil
Shopping cart wheels (axles)	light grease
Skates (bearings)	light oil
Tape player (head)	special formula or isopropyl alcohol
Typewriter (carriage track)	wax
Zippers	special grease stick or wax

Lucite: Lucite, an acrylic plastic, (and the similar Plexiglas) has become an important decorative medium and is an attractive item of contemporary furniture. It is highly durable, can resist hammer blows and is practically flameproof. But it is also susceptible to scratches from both sharp objects and abrasive cleaners, can become dulled from exposure to the weather and is affected by both excessive heat and certain chemicals.

Clean the plastic by washing with warm water and detergent, rinse and dry. Do not use very hot water, which may soften the material and possibly cause it to change shape. Light scratches can be covered up with an application of colorless wax; deeper scratches may be smoothed out by rubbing with Brasso abrasive paste. If scratches remain, special buffing equipment used in commercial shops can restore original appearance.

Lucite is basically colorless and transparent, but also comes tinted in various shades and in opaque colors. (See also *Acrylics*, page 25.)

Luggage: Though subjected to scuffs, impact stresses and other abuses, your luggage can be kept presentably neat by proper cleaning. Methods vary according to the type of covering and lining.

ALUMINUM: Molded, lightweight aluminum cases are easiest to clean. Use a chrome metal polish applied with a dauber cloth and rub to a high luster with a pad.

FABRIC: Linen, cotton, denim, canvas and other fabric coverings for luggage should be treated like clothing fabric. Clean them with soap and water, use spot remover on stains. Dry them thoroughly before storing. Spray on a water or stain repellent such as Scotchgard if desired. Protect fabric-covered luggage from mildewing.

FIBERGLASS: Clean with soapy pad, rinse and dry. Use fine steel wool on scuffs and scratches. Special pastes (Sudbury's Gel) restore luster.

HARDWARE: Do not oil luggage locks or hinges. Rub scratches or rust with steel wool or emery cloth. Spray on a protective coating of lacquer or apply clear nail polish. Lubricate the casters if your luggage is equipped with this roll-along convenience. Lubricate the zipper each month or so to prevent troublesome snags.

LEATHER: Clean with saddle soap, let dry, then rub in paste wax or neutral shoe cream. Brown leather can be darkened by applying several coats of lemon oil. Colored leathers should be cleaned with mild soap, conditioned with cream type shoe polish. Dry thoroughly; store in a cool, dry place. (See also *Leather*, page 102; *Mildew*, page 112.)

LININGS: Usually made of synthetic-fiber fabric, these are sponged with soap and water. Spraying with aerosol waterproofing compound helps repel lipstick and other greasy stains, but not much can be done to protect against nail polish spills.

VINYL: Soap and water usually are sufficient to deal with average soiling, but if dirt spots remain, use a special vinyl cleaner (see *Vinyl Tops* in *Automobile Cleaning* section, page 35.) or use ammonia, diluted 2 tablespoons in 1 pint of water. Apply liquid wax when dry.

Lycra: A DuPont product similar to nylon, but with exceptional elasticity, high strength and flexing life greater than conventional elastic. See *Spandex,* page 157, for care and laundering instruction.

Marble: Wiping with a damp cloth usually is sufficient to retain the luster of this decorative and practical stone. Wash with a mild detergent to remove dirt that has dulled the surface, scrubbing with a fiber brush if needed, then apply a clear, non-yellowing wax.

Stains and etch marks are caused by acids like fruit juices, tomato products and vinegar; also organic substances such as wet bark, flowers and dyes from colored textiles. Marble absorbs oil stains from such foods as butter, cream, peanut butter, mustard and salad oils. Rust stains come commonly from steel wool or contact with ferrous objects. Use coasters under beverage glasses, place mats at snack servings, to avoid staining of a marble table.

To clear up a stained spot, first try rubbing with a mild cleanser and felt pad. If further treatment is required try a poultice (a white blotter or paper towel with powdered household cleanser or chalk moistened and placed over the stain.) The purpose is to leach out the staining substance. For an organic stain, soak the poultice with hydrogen peroxide, household ammonia or hair shampoo. Oil stains are removed by wetting the poultice with acetone (nail polish remover), benzene (lighter fluid) or other such solvents. Rust stains are treated by soaking with commercial rust remover, tin oxide or whiting.

Leave the poultice in place for several hours at least and repeat the process with a new application if traces of the stain remain.

The glossy polish of marble sometimes may be restored to damaged edges by rubbing with a nonscratching powder cleanser and fine emery cloth, or the use of an electric hand grinder with an abrasive stone. Restoration of chipped edges on contoured marble or statuary requires the services of a marble fabricator who has the required equipment.

Mattress: The best protection for your mattress is a plasticized, fitted mattress cover, which will require only an occasional wiping with a slightly damp cloth between regular launderings. Wash the cover according to label instructions. A quilted surface pad, preferred by some, also will be satisfactory.

Mattresses may be cleaned by brisk brushing with a whisk broom or by vacuuming. Light washing is done with almost dry detergent suds brushed over a small area at a time and wiped off quickly.

Latex (foam rubber) mattresses need not be turned, but others should be turned over, top to bottom, and turned around end to end, every couple of months in the first year and every 6 months thereafter.

Air any mattress near open windows each time the linen is changed, but do not expose a foam rubber mattress to direct sunlight.

Microwave Ovens: Wipe up spills around the door seal, door surface or oven frame if they occur. Keep the filter free of soil and grease. Make sure the filter is in place before operating the oven. Use only cooking utensils recommended for the microwave oven, including those made of porcelain, glass, wood, paper or plastic—not metal.

Mildew: Mold spores, always present in the air, flourish in damp and warm places where the air is stagnant, causing dark green stains, musty odors and often considerable damage to clothing, furniture, books and the house itself. Mildew is most common in muggy summer months, and year-round in high-humidity areas.

Mildew occurs mostly in basements, crawl spaces, closets and on exterior siding on the shady side of the house. Shoes and leather-bound books are favorite objects of attack, but all fabrics of natural fibers, upholstered furniture and damp articles are susceptible.

The air conditioner is an effective weapon against mildew; in addition to cooling, it draws moisture out of the air. A humidistat regulates the air conditioner (separately from the thermostat) so that humidity is maintained at a constant level.

There's more to mildew defenses, however, than just turning on the air conditioner. These steps can be taken to ward off mildew damage and deal with any occurrence:

1. *Control dampness.* Provide an outside vent to remove the steam and moisture from a clothes dryer. Caulk joints in the house walls, point up any crumbled mortar in brickwork, restore grouting on bathroom tiles, prune shrubbery that keeps the ground damp around foundation walls and correct any water seepage into the basement or from roof gutters. Insulate exposed cold water pipes from condensation. Keep windows shut on damp summer nights, raise shades and open windows on dry sunny afternoons.

2. *Dry the air.* Warm air holds more moisture. Keep the air conditioner on automatic setting to maintain normal relative humidity when you're away from home on vacation. Another device is the dehumidifier, which can draw gallons of water out of the basement air in a day, but be sure to empty its tank regularly if it doesn't drain directly into the sewer. Useful too are chemical driers, like copper sulphate which absorbs mois-

ture, and calcium chloride, which precipitates and condenses water (Damp Rid). Containers with the chemicals are placed in closets and pantries and must be emptied of water regularly.

3. *Keep things clean and moisture free.* Soil and grease provide nutrients for mildew organisms. Synthetic-fiber fabrics, for example, are not in themselves subject to mildew, but any dirt or soil present on the fabric attracts spores. Wardrobes and drawers should be emptied and cleaned occasionally. Never leave clothes or linens lying around while damp, and spread out shower curtains to dry, instead of leaving them bunched up. Wipe dry the shower panels after each use—an easy way is to draw a rubber squeegee across the stall surfaces. An all-plastic squeegee (Shower-Dri, Ardmore) will avoid scratching the wall surfaces. Store shoes, handbags and other leather goods in dry and cool places.

4. *Be alert to fungus signs.* Closets usually do not have heater or air conditioner ducts, and some of the walls may be on the exterior side. Moisture from warm air condenses on the cooler wall, and with the closet's darkness and stagnant air, provides prime conditions for mildew. A tiny fan in the closet can keep the air fresh, while a small lamp (a 25-watt bulb will help) can provide dry heat and light. Routinely, spray the closet with mildew germicide (Lysol, Listerine) and place in it a cup of moisture-drawing calcium chloride.

5. *Remove odors.* Sprinkle chlorinated lime, purchased at garden- and building-supply dealers, on the basement floor to remove musty odors. For bathrooms and showers, scrub surfaces with chlorine bleach, ½ cup in 1 gallon of water, then spray surfaces regularly—every couple of weeks is recommended—with a mildew-inhibitor spray, or wipe down the surfaces with a germicidal detergent.

6. *Restoring Garments.* All mildew-affected articles should first be wiped or brushed to remove the mold, but do this outdoors to prevent scattering the spores in the house. Launder or dry clean. Treat persistent stains with a mixture of lemon juice and salt, spread the clothes in sunlight to bleach or use diluted chlorine bleach on the moistened garment (see *Laundering,* page 9.)

Stains can be removed from shoes, handbags, books and similar objects by wiping with a cloth dipped into rubbing alcohol; or use a commercial mildew cleaner (X-14) containing calcium hypochlorite as the active ingredient, in spray form or with an applicator sponge.

To dry wallpaper, raise the heat of the room as needed for the purpose. Wipe the wallcovering with a soapy pad, bleach out any stains with lemon juice or chlorine solution. Spray with germicidal Lysol or Listerine. (See also *Stains,* page 158.)

Mirrors: Wipe with a soft cloth moistened with diluted vinegar or ammonia, or use a glass spray (Windex, Glass Wax, etc.). Dry with a paper towel or lintless cloth, polishing to avoid streaks. An old-time favorite, still widely used, is Bon Ami in cake form, which dries to a white powder that is slightly abrasive so that the polishing that clears away the powder produces a sparkling cleanliness.

Antifogging film is achieved by wiping with a soapy sponge, but be careful to prevent water getting on the silvered back of the mirror or seeping inside a wooden frame. The silvering at the back of a mirror can be protected with a coating of clear shellac.

Moths: The tiny larvae feed voraciously on wool, furs, carpets, linens—anything of animal or vegetable origin—and are especially fond of fine cashmere sweaters and the felt dampers in pianos. They shun synthetics such as nylon and rayon, but fabrics having some wool in the yarn are vulnerable. Keep cleaned garments in closets or drawers with plenty of naphthalene flakes. Spray areas with an anti-moth insecticide. Chlordane and DDT are both very effective, but chlordane has been banned for private use in some localities, and DDT has been removed from sale in the United States.

Reliance on paradichlorobenzene (para) alone may not be sufficient. A systematic preventive and control program provides the most dependable protection against moth infestation. See listing in Booklet Section of USDA Bulletin #113.

Nail Polish: Acetone is the solvent used for removing nail polish, as noted previously, and it also will dissolve lacquer, which is the coating used on much furniture today. Take the necessary precautions when using acetone not to damage other surfaces. Acetone is highly flammable.

Non-Stick Pans: See *Cookware: Teflon-Coated,* page 61.

Nylon: This strongest of manmade fibers is widely used for garments, hosiery, tents, fishing lines and many other everyday products. In solid form, the nylon plastic serves for bearings, gears and such household items as casters, drawer glides, brush bristles, kitchen utensils, even drinking glasses.

Nylon fabrics have the great advantage of resistance to soiling, and fresh stains usually yield to just sponging with water. But white nylon fabrics tend to become discolored when laundered with heavily soiled or dyed garments. For washing instructions, see *Laundering Permanent-Press Garments,* page 15.

Nylon plastic utensils, brushes and other items are not vulnerable to most cleaning chemicals nor to hot water, so may be placed in the dishwasher and even boiled.

Odors: Ample ventilation, aided by an exhaust fan or electric air purifier, helps remove offensive odors to keep the home pleasantly fresh-smelling. Air "sweeteners"—the aerosol, plunger bottle or wick types—mask undesirable odors with their own lemon, peppermint or chlorophyl fragrances.

Lemon juice and vinegar are two old-fashioned and still widely used deodorizers.

Good housekeeping is the best method to avoid unpleasant odors by eliminating their sources. Wash out garbage cans, spray with germicidal cleanser, line them with plastic bags, dispose of garbage promptly. Air bedding and garments regularly. Wash the refrigerator interior, empty and clean pantry and closets regularly.

Various old-time methods still serve well for specific conditions. Overcome stale tobacco odor by placing open bowls of vinegar in the room. Cinnamon spilled on a hot stove will disguise the odor of burned food. Add a few walnuts to the pot with cabbage to reduce the characteristic odor. Soaking fish in boiling salt water for a few minutes is said to prevent the usual odor while cooking. A saucer of vinegar exposed in the kitchen is sufficient to minimize the cooking odors of broccoli, brussels sprouts, cauliflower. Deodorize Tupperware and similar plastic food containers by placing them in the freezer for a couple of hours.

In the refrigerator, an open container of baking soda or pieces of charcoal will help keep it fresh-smelling without altering the taste of stored food. Oil of wintergreen also is recommended for this purpose.

Kerosene and gasoline odor on your hands or clothing can be neutralized by rubbing with vinegar or a strong salt solution; rubbing with a piece of cut lemon can remove onion scent from your fingers. To freshen a room quickly when guests are on the way, light the fireplace logs and toss in a handful of juniper berries.

Keep a supply of scented soap in your linen closet, in stored suitcases and storage drawers. The wrappers of soap cakes also will serve well in those places to maintain a pleasant fragrance.

Other items that counteract odors or produce a pleasant scent of their own are:

pine cones	vinegar
cinnamon	incense-various
oil of wintergreen	lemon

herbs	perfumes
gin	bathsalts
hickory or cedar chips in fireplace	potpourri (an open jar of various fragrant flowers, herbs, spices
peppermint	and oils, mixed to provide a
sachet of lavender	desired aroma)
cedar oil	ice cubes

MOTHBALL CRYSTALS: The reek of paradichlorobenzene crystals can be counteracted with a mixture of equal parts rubbing alcohol and lemon juice or vinegar. Moisten a sponge or cloth pad with the solution, wipe down the interior of drawers, closets and luggage as necessary.

NEW PAINT: Most house decorating these days is done with latex paint, which has the grace to be odorless and quick-drying. Oil paint still is used on occasion, however, and it's the turpentine thinner—or solvent—that releases the obnoxious fumes. Keep windows open and exhaust fan on, limit exposure to the fumes.

One means of overcoming paint odor is said to be cutting up a couple of large onions into a pail of water. Burning dried orange peels in a metal ashtray, or better still, lighting some cologne, also can clear the paint odor.

SKUNK: The musky odor may be brought into your home by the pet dog after a run in the fields. Some sources, who are supposed to know, advocate tomato juice, applied liberally to the animal's coat, as an antidote. Follow with a regular wash with soap and water. There's nothing much that can be done about skunk odor that pervades a neighborhood except to wait until time has worked its magic. (See *Mildew,* page 112, for details on damp and musty odors.)

Oriental Rugs: See *Carpets and Rugs: Oriental Rugs,* page 51.

Orlon: This acrylic fiber, a DuPont product manufactured from petroleum and natural gas, is processed in a reactor vessel to form a polymer which is dissolved and spun into a filament. In texture, Orlon ranges from soft to crisp, and may be bulky or fine. Widely used for sweaters, slacks, dresses, draperies and for pile fabrics used to line outerwear garments. The fiber is durable, quick drying, resistant to wrinkles, mildewing and moths. Care and washing procedures are the same as for polyester, but read and follow the specific label instructions.

Ovens: See *Ranges,* page 136; also *Microwave Ovens,* page 111.

Painted Walls: The description usually is to "wash down" a wall, but actually the correct technique is to start at the bottom and work up. Streaks of dirt thus do not leave tracks on the lower wall which would be most difficult to wash away. Cover the adjacent floor area with newspapers or a drop cloth.

Use a wall detergent (Mr. Clean, Pine Sol) in hot or warm water. Apply with a sponge. Wash a section at a time until it looks clean. Rinse with fresh water from a different pail (even if the detergent container says it's not necessary), change the rinse water occasionally so dirt isn't just smeared around. Gather and dispose of the wet newspapers promptly to prevent soaking the floor area.

Walls tend to become especially dirty around light switches and doorknobs. No need for an overall cleaning—just a quick wiping with a sponge and soap or liquid wall-cleaner does the job.

For exterior walls, see *House Siding,* page 93.

Painting

EXTERIOR PAINTING: Reach for a scrub brush instead of a paint-brush when clapboard siding appears drab. The walls may be simply dirty; you'll be surprised, most likely, to find under the grime that the original coating is in sound condition, the color still bright. If the exterior walls were painted within three or four years, a fresh coating usually is not needed; in fact, as previously noted, it's actually harmful to pile on fresh layers before the existing paint has weathered sufficiently to both reduce its thickness and form an effective base for repainting. Too many coats of paint create a thick film that pulls away from the wall by its own weight, the cause of much paint failure. Conditions such as peeling, blistering and checking require prompt attention, however, and their repair usually means repainting at least one side of the house to avoid a patchy appearance.

There are important advantages to a schedule in which just one side of the house is painted each year. In that way, each side receives a new coating every fifth year; there will be little noticeable fading contrast in adjoining walls. It's best to retain the same color for each application, and that may require buying a sufficient quantity of paint at one time; unopened cans of paint are easily stored until needed.

Just flushing the walls with plain water from the garden hose may be sufficient. For dirty walls, use a pail of liquid detergent solution and a long-handled brush, the kind used for washing cars. A hose brush with a detergent-dispensing valve, also available at auto supply stores, will make the job easier, rinsing away the dirty water simultaneously.

Where possible, work from the bottom up, so that the lower surface is clean and water running down from higher up won't create streaks that will be difficult to remove. It's a good idea, for this reason, to keep the washed sections wet at all times. Wipe the windowsills first from above to lessen the dirt runoff. Stubborn spots will need attention with a hand scrubbing-brush.

Most homes will not need complete overall scrubbing, just particular spots under windowsills and on the side walls directly below the chimney. When you are spot-scrubbing, however, take the necessary steps to avoid streaking as described previously. Window screens also can cause considerable runoff of dirty water—it's best to take them down to be flushed off separately, laying them flat on the driveway and hosing them down.

After scrubbing, spray the walls with the garden hose to flush away all the detergent before it can dry on the surface. Then examine the exterior walls for signs of mildew stains, particularly sections under the eaves that are sheltered from sunlight, on the underside of roof gutters, and along the foundation where there are damp areas of soil. (See *Mildew*, page 112, for methods of treatment.)

Prompt wall maintenance and paint touch-up can put off a complete paint job for another year. Check all house joints around doors, windows, dormers—apply new caulking where needed. Scrape off loose paint, chipped spots and blisters, sand around the bare spots to taper the edges (called "feathering") and wipe away the sanding dust. Apply a primer coat (usually the paint used for the surface also serves as the primer) having the necessary sealer and adhesion properties built into the formulation. After thorough drying of the primer, touch up the spots with a matching paint, preferably some that was saved from the original job.

PAINTING TOOL CLEANUP: Brushes, rollers, pans and other painting tools can be kept in serviceable condition indefinitely if completely cleaned immediately after use—while the paint is still fresh—and if stored properly. Latex paint washes off readily with water. Oil-based paints require a mineral solvent (turps, etc.) which may not always be handy or convenient to use. But it's not always necessary to clean the tools if the painting is to be continued the next day. Wrap wet oil-paint brushes tightly in aluminum foil or polyethylene sheeting and they will stay pliable for a day or two.

While latex paint can be kept soft temporarily by immersing the tools in water, it's not advisable to depend on that course. If the painting is interrupted briefly, for mealtime, say, a quick rinsing under a water tap will prevent the latex drying in that time, and painting can be resumed with the wet roller or brushes.

Cleaning a brush or roller, whether with latex or oil paint, is not a 1-2-3 routine. Instead, thorough cleaning is essential —even the slightest spot of matted paint makes a brush or roller useless. Similarly, all the other equipment that was used must be washed—ladder, steps, roller core, paint tray, putty-knife blade, etc.

1. *Rollers.* Start roller cleanup by pulling the cloth cover

off its metal core. Rinse off latex paint with running water, under a faucet, if possible, otherwise in a pan of fresh water. Squeeze out most of the paint, then wash in soapy water. Encircle the roller core with your fingers, move back and forth over the cover until no more paint is squeezed out. Rinse in fresh water, then stand the roller on end for drying. You'll be surprised to note that quite a lot of paint has remained in the roller nap to seep down to the bottom—that should indicate the extent of washing needed. Clean the roller core and handle, also the pan and all other tools that have been used, in soapy water. Rinse and dry with paper toweling.

Oil paint requires soaking the roller cover in a solvent (varnolene or benzene) to soften and dilute concentrated blobs of paint. Wear rubber gloves if you are sensitive to the mineral solvents; take adequate precautions because of flammability. When all paint has been removed, wash the roller cover and core separately with detergent to remove stickiness; rinse and dry. All the other painting tools are also cleaned with solvent.

2. *Brushes.* After using with oil or alkyd paint, stroke the brush across old newspapers, or another surface that can be discarded, to remove as much paint as possible. Follow with several dippings in mineral spirits (varnolene or benzene) up above the metal ferrule, squeezing out paint. Finally, wash in trisodium phosphate, or laundry detergent; rinse in clear water. Swing the brush through the air to remove excess water, wait until dry, then wrap the bristles in kraft paper held with a rubber band or cord to keep the bristles straight.

Brushes used with latex paint are cleaned by the same procedure described earlier for latex rollers.

A brush used for applying shellac should be kept solely for that purpose. Alcohol is the solvent for shellac, but you're not likely to restore a brush that has been used for shellac to original condition with either alcohol or ammonia. However, if the brush is needed again for shellacking, alcohol softens the bristles, no matter how long since the brush has been used. Use the inexpensive methanol alcohol, purchased at paint-supply and hardware stores. Caution: The alcohol is both poisonous and flammable.

Only lacquer thinner (acetone) will effectively clean tools used with lacquer. Just dip and wipe several times until the color disappears; then wash the brush in soapy water. Do the cleaning outdoors to avoid inhaling the lacquer fumes and as protection against the high flash-fire potential of lacquer thinner.

Hardened paintbrushes sometimes can be restored by overnight soaking in a 15 percent solution of trisodium phosphate (TSP) or one of the commercial brush cleaners. Suspend the brush, preferably with a thin wood dowel through a hole in the handle, into the solution so the bristles do not rest on the bottom of the container and the liquid level is just above the metal ferrule edge. When the bristles begin to soften, work them apart gently with a putty knife. A nylon-bristle brush can be boiled for cleaning, if necessary, to soften the bristles. Natural-bristle brushes cannot be boiled.

spatters: Latex paint, while still fresh, wipes off readily with just a damp cloth, but may leave discoloring spots on polished furniture which can be removed by rubbing with a cleaner polish or rewaxing. Dried spots on floor or furniture usually can be rubbed off with fine-grit sandpaper or steel wool.

Remove oil paint before it dries by wiping with the solvent for that type of paint. Dried paint may require treatment with trisodium phosphate (TSP) or a paste type paint remover. Try first scraping paint from a hard surface with a knife blade.

special formula paints: Some plastic enamels are made with specific odor-free thinners, which usually are the only solvents that can be used to clean the painting tools. The label on the enamel can should tell you which cleaner to use.

paint stripping: In the home, use only the nonflammable, water-rinse, paste type paint removers which are, nonetheless, highly toxic and require ventilation, preferably aided by a fan, to drive off fumes.

Paint stripping is, at best, a very messy job. Place plenty of

newspapers on the floor, protect nearby furniture with polyethylene sheeting, wrap papers with the scraped-off paint
muck securely for discarding and wash all tools in soapy
water.

Enamels and varnish are removed in the same way as oil
paint; shellac is softened by alcohol; lacquer is taken off with
acetone. These solvents are volatile, so use caution.

Latex paint cannot be stripped with a chemical remover,
only scraped off with a blade or sander. It's easier to just paint
over on top of the old coat after correcting any deterioration
in the surface.

Trisodium phosphate (TSP) is an inexpensive paint
remover for large surfaces, preferably horizontal, on which
the paint coatings are not too thick. Dissolve a pound of TSP
(available as Soilax, Spic 'n Span) in a gallon of hot water to
make a strong solution, apply with a brush, wait at least half
an hour for the paint to soften and scrape with a broad putty
knife. Be sure to protect the floor with wads of newspapers
to catch dripping solution.

Rinse thoroughly with a sponge and clear water, dry the
wood promptly with toweling to avoid raising the grain.
(Caution: do not allow the TSP solution to drip on painted
surfaces that are to remain intact.) Wash off any spills immediately.

For vertical applications on walls and furniture, make a
thick paste of 1 part TSP, 2 parts whiting and just a sufficient amount of water; apply a fairly thick coat evenly
over the surface with a putty knife. After half an hour,
scrape off the old finish, rinse thoroughly. Some popular
paint remover brands are Red Devil, Dap, No-Flame,
Savogran, Wonder Water Wash. (See Part 3 for sources of
further information.)

Paneling: Treat the surface of Marlite and other finished wall
paneling similarly to wooden furniture; clean by wiping with
a mild, low-luster furniture polish. Avoid scouring with
cleansers and strong soaps which may dull the finish. Before
using a commercial panel cleaner, test it on an inconspicuous
area of the paneling. Do not apply adhesive tape or stickers

to the face of the panel. A protective wax coating (Pledge) will make dusting easier.

Patio Furniture: Lawn and patio furniture normally require some maintenance attention after each season of use. Faded colors, torn seat-webbing, rust-frozen chaise pivots, chipped paint and sun-bleached awnings should be repaired to maintain the usually expensive furniture in good condition, giving it a new lease on life.

At the start of the season, scrub down all the furniture and umbrellas with a soft brush and detergent, flush with the garden hose, dry with old terry towels. Look for and replace any missing bolts or fasteners (use rustproof metal, of course), reweave with new plastic webbing any torn strips, tighten screws in wood furniture, peen loosened rivets (use two hammers, one serving as the anvil behind the rivet). Stains on cushions, umbrellas or awnings can be removed with an eraser-type cleaner such as Rubgum. Redwood will be more attractive if treated annually with a penetrating sealer, coating the end grain, particularly including the bottom of the legs which are in direct contact with the patio ground. (See also *Lawn Umbrellas,* page 102.)

Pearls: The best thing for pearls is just to wear them. Between times, though, keep them in a box lined with velvet or other soft material; rub occasionally with a dry chamois. Some pearl devotees claim that storing them with rice helps keep their luster. More dependable, though, is professional cleaning and restringing at least once a year. Restringing is essential to avoid sudden loss; make sure that string is properly knotted. Avoid the tendency of some to twist pearls while wearing them.

Permanent Press: Preshaped polyester knits are wrinkle-resistant, retain the original shape after laundering or cleaning, won't shrink or stretch when properly heat-set. But the fabric has an affinity for oily soil, thus requires frequent laundering.

Machine wash small loads in warm or cool water, except for heavily soiled garments, which will require a hot-water wash and the attendant special attention that means. Do not mix colors—wash all whites in one load, colorfast items in another. Perborate (peroxide) bleach may be used on all synthetic textiles, but follow label direction for effect on color.

Avoid quick temperature changes, as when shifting garments from washing machine to dryer. Use the permanent-press setting on washer and dryer. Tumble dry for 10 minutes or so after turning off the heater, for gradual cooling, then remove the garments promptly. If allowed to remain until the clothing becomes wrinkled, do the drying cycle over again.

Dacron, nylon and other permanent-press garments may be dry cleaned, unless stated otherwise on the label. (See also section on *Laundering,* page 9)

Pest Control: Freedom from insects in the home is purchased by good housekeeping. Cleanliness is the first step in discouraging pests: food kept in tightly closed containers, preferably glass jars; dishes promptly washed and dried; garbage disposed of quickly; closets kept dry, airy and vacuum cleaned. Screened barriers effectively keep out mosquitoes, flies and other flying insects, but the main defense against ants, weevils and roaches is both exterior and interior spraying with potent insecticides at regular intervals.

There are two basic types of insecticide sprays for home use. Those labeled "space spray" kill flying insects like mosquitoes almost immediately. The "surface" or "residual" sprays leave a coating on floor and walls that is effective for weeks and is lethal to insects like ants, roaches and bugs that crawl over the surface. (See also *Moths,* page 114.)

No campaign against household pests will be long successful without attention to these basic conditions that will prevent or control an insect invasion:

1. Close all openings as far as possible. Seal wall cracks, no matter how tiny; screen frames must fit tightly; caulk all wall joints; provide interlock closure seals at door sills.

2. Sanitation and good housekeeping are key prerequisites to preventive measures. Clean out closets and pantries, vacuum regularly to destroy insect nests.

3. Protection against pantry pests includes sealing all cartons and tightly closing food jars. Wash up soiled dishes promptly; keep garbage in covered plastic bags; dispose of garbage frequently. Close covers on toilet seats to limit access to water.

4. Use proper insecticides at adequate intervals. Spray with long-lasting repellent, including the home exterior. Pay attention to safe and effective applications.

Many insecticides that are effective in protecting our homes and gardens against obnoxious insects are also toxic to humans and pets, and some are flammable. Safe use of insecticides is the responsibility of the householder. Store them properly, always tightly closed, and out of the way of children.

Commercial insecticides purchased under brand names are required by law to specify on the labels the insecticides they contain, what kinds of insects they are to be used against, basic instructions for their use, and precautions in handling. Many insecticides have long technical names; often just a slight difference in spelling can indicate a totally different function or capability, so some labels also give the common name by which the insecticide is known.

The most readily available insecticides and their effective uses are:

1. *Chlordane.* This chemical is very effective against ants and termites. Diluted to a 2 percent solution in kerosene or water, it is sprinkled around the house perimeter, or brushed on foundation walls. Do not use as a spray. It is extremely toxic. Do not use indoors. Chlordane sales have been sharply restricted in many communities.

2. *DDT.* Sale of this very effective insecticide has been banned by federal regulation, although the restriction has been lifted on occasion to meet emergency conditions. Highly toxic to humans.

3. *Lindane.* Used in 5 percent solutions for residual applications. Hazardous when used as a spray.

4. *Methoxychlor.* Less toxic than DDT, kills flies that have become resistant to DDT.

5. *Pyrethrum.* A natural product extracted from pyrethrum blossoms, it is used as a spray or powder against various domestic and plant insects. Must be applied frequently as the effectiveness is not long-lasting.

ANTS: They go big for candies, spilled sugar and cereals, loose crumbs and the like. Store food in tightly capped glass jars or sealed plastic bags. Wipe up any food spills, especially of sweets, promptly. Monthly, or more frequently if necessary, spray with a suitable insecticide (landane, malathion, diazinon) to keep the pests under control. Spray along the baseboard around the kitchen and pantry, not neglecting the rear of the refrigerator, inside closets and cabinets. Window screens don't keep out ants—they get in under doors and through any tiny openings. Positive results are obtained by spraying the outside perimeter of your home with chlordane. This is a highly toxic chemical which must be handled with proper precaution; in some states, the use of chlordane is limited to professional exterminators, and it is not available for purchase by the public.

CENTIPEDES: These favor damp basements and destroy other insects but are themselves objectional invaders of the home. Pyrethrum powder, sprinkled at suspected breeding places, provides adequate control.

GNATS: Camphor is an effective preventative against gnats and also the best cure for their stings. You'd find it difficult, however, to hold the camphor in a way to obtain protection; fortunately, however, there are more convenient repellents that are simply sprayed on clothing or harmlessly on the skin. Make sure to read the label instructions.

ROACHES: The first step in the war against this nasty pest is strict control of food and water; that is, no crumbs left on table or floor, all cereal packages tightly sealed, dishes promptly washed, garbage cans emptied and sanitized and kept tightly closed, dishes carefully dried, no open containers of water left around.

Both contact killer sprays and residual (long-lasting) insecticides are used in efforts to eliminate any infestation and prevent a recurrence. Sodium fluoride and pyrethrum are

effective insecticides against roaches. Spray along base-
boards, at any crack in the wall, behind appliances and the
sink, at pipe openings in walls, and along door sills. Since
window screens are never snug enough in their frames to
block insect entry completely, they should be treated with a
residual-type insecticide, either sprayed or brushed on.

Research has found that boric acid (known also as boracic
acid) is a good means for getting rid of roaches. Boric acid
does not have an unpleasant odor and is not poisonous, although it may have a toxic effect on pets.

Roaches are not fit for human habitation. Stamp them out!

scorpions: This member of the spider family occurs in the Gulf
states and in Kentucky, Tennessee and Missouri. Its sting is
dangerous and may even be fatal to young children and to
adults who are sensitive to its toxin. Insecticides recommended by the USDA are lindane and chlorpyrifos, at the
dosage of 0.3 micrograms per square centimeter of area for
lindane and 4 micrograms for chlorpyrifos (1 microgram per
centimeter equals 1 milligram per square foot). Tests have
shown that DDT is relatively ineffective for control of scorpions, even at very high dosage.

silverfish: A warm, dry basement or attic is a likely breeding
place of an infestation. The insect feeds on paper, starchy
fabrics and rayon, because it likes the cellulose content. Use
commercial residual sprays on any suspected source area.

spiders, carpet beetles: Frequent and careful vacuum cleaning
is the best means of preventing or eliminating infestations of
spiders and carpet beetles. The tiny beetle hides inside furniture, pianos, radios, other dark places where dust collects.
Spiders of course spread their webs wherever they're not
disturbed. Chlordane, Dieldrin and lindane are the recommended control agents.

termites: These antlike insects, which bore into the inner core
of house framing, have their nests outside the house. They
usually are not detected until after the damage is done. One
sign of their presence is an earthen tube leading across a
foundation wall, or over a pipe or pillar, through which the

termites cross from one place to another, thus avoiding daylight. Occasionally, a swarm of young adults will emerge, leaving a debris of shucked wings. This may provide the clue enabling you to trace them to their breeding place. Licensed exterminators use insecticides, mostly chlordane, that are not available to the consumer, and usually guarantee the termite control for a number of years. But don't be convinced without evidence of termites. Be on guard when selecting an exterminator to avoid excessive charges for superficial protection against something you can't see or check on. Incidentally, termite damage to your home, even if extensive and costly, is not deductible as a casualty loss for income tax purposes, because of the long-term, if insidious, nature of the attack.

Phonograph Records: Anti-static solutions help protect your records, keep grooves dust-free for better performance. Wipe records occasionally (some audio aficionados do this each time a record is played) with a soft, chamoislike cloth, dampened slightly with an anti-static solution or with a special brush made for that purpose. Apply the cloth or brush in a circular motion along the grooves, not across them, while holding the record with its edge pressed against your body to avoid fingermarks.

Anti-static solutions are sold at record and electronics shops. You can make your own by combining 1 part ethylene glycol with 4 parts water. Very little is needed. Store in a tightly stoppered bottle.

Dirt-embedded records sometimes can be restored by washing with a mild detergent in lukewarm water and drying with a soft, lint-free cloth. Replace records in their jackets after use, store in vertical position and away from the room heater to avoid warping. Do not leave records stacked on the player changer.

Phonograph Speakers: The cloth facing needs occasional dusting. Use the small circular brush attachment of your vacuum cleaner, adjusted for gentle air flow so the cloth won't be pulled outward. The plastic-coated speaker case, when dulled by a coating of film, can be restored to its fresh appearance by wiping with a moistened cloth or sponge. Plain water does the job most times; no need for detergents or polishing agents. Use a furniture cleaner like Pledge when necessary.

Photographs: Protect photo prints in individual clear plastic sleeves of a bound album or similar container that keeps pictures from curling and cracking. Prints also can be laminated to a backing board with Kodak dry-mounting tissue, applied with a hot household iron, or McDonald special adhesive, both available at camera stores. Do not use ordinary library paste, which may cause blistering and curling.

Soiled prints can be cleaned by washing them in warm water, then dipping in a flattening solution (Kodak.) Dry by pressing between large white blotters. If you have the negatives, replace cracked and torn old pictures with new prints; otherwise it's possible to have the pictures repaired by a photo retoucher using a special air brush. Copies are first made from the old prints and then are retouched. The new prints then made will be almost equal in clarity to the originals.

Piano: This combination of graceful furniture and fine musical instrument deserves the most devoted attention. Proper placement away from heating radiators and windows to limit temperature changes, regular tuning, polishing and cleaning and a consistent relative humidity level of 50 percent in the house, all contribute to good maintenance.

Ivory keys are cleaned by wiping with a cloth slightly dampened with a salt and lemon juice solution (be sure the fluid does not seep down between keys), then wiped dry. Ivory tends to discolor in the dark, so keep the keyboard lid open. Keys that have yellowed can be removed for repolishing, or replaced with plastic tabs that are whiter, easier to clean and will not darken with age.

The felt on hammers and dampers is vulnerable to moths. Vacuum-clean the harp, strings and mechanism regularly. During the spring and summer months it is wise to place a quantity of mothballs (naphthalene) or para flakes in the interior, but not directly on the strings—rather, put down a couple of layers of newspaper and cover the paper with the

flakes. (Although some piano tuners advise against keeping
newspapers inside and favor just keeping the top down.)

The piano case is treated like other fine furniture with the
object of preserving the finish. Keep it clean and highly polished (see *Furniture,* page 81).

STICKY KEYS: Wipe the sides as well as the top of each key with
a damp cloth; alcohol may be used for this purpose. To replace any key tab that has worked loose, spread a thin layer
of rubber cement on the back of the tab and also on the key
itself; wait until cement has dried; line up the tab precisely
on the key, lower into position and press down hard for a
moment or so. The tab will be immediately bonded to the
key. But leave this cementing to a professional piano tuner
if you're not positive that you can put tabs on in perfectly
uniform alignment.

Pillows: Laundering, by hand or in the machine, is difficult and
time-consuming because of the care required for drying and
fluffing. The use of cotton or tightly woven polyester covers
reduces the need for pillow washings to restore freshness,
remove soil and eliminate odor. Check the pillow labels for
washing instructions.

Pillows of feather, down and polyester fillers can be
laundered by hand in a tub or the washing machine; pillows with foam rubber or kapok fillers become lumpy and
should not be laundered. Dacron-filled pillows can be
freshened by running them in the dryer at highest heat.
Feather pillows are best laundered by transferring the
feathers to a separate, oversize muslin bag, the opening of
which is then sewn tightly so no feathers slip through in
the washing. The filled muslin bag is washed in a tub with
warm detergent solution sloshed through the feathers for
4 to 8 minutes. Rinse thoroughly in the same manner,
with at least three changes of water. Hang the bag on a
line to dry or place in the dryer, set at maximum heat for
the longest cycle. Stop dryer occasionally, shake and fluff
the pillows. Pillows must be dried completely to prevent
mildewing.

Pipe: See *Water Pipe,* page 181.

Plastic Laminate: Of all the surface finishes in the home, the easiest to clean and most durable is the thin melamine-coated sheeting of which the most prominent brand is Formica. For many years Formica was the surface material for nearly all kitchen counters. It is widely used now for cabinet and desk tops, bathroom vanities, even wall panels. Its surface can closely resemble fine woods in both color and grain pattern and it also comes in many solid colors and patterns.

Cleaning usually takes just a swipe with a damp cloth or sponge. Use a mild cleanser like liquid Soft Scrub or Ivory to remove food spots, crayon, smudges and other soils.

The plastic is resistant to stains and boiling water, but scorching can result from pots and pans placed straight from the oven or stove; use a trivet or asbestos pad. The textured type of plastic may be somewhat more difficult to clean with just soap. A new spray cleaner by Formica lifts dirt from such textured or satin surfaces, and will remove minor stains. If the stain persists after two or three tries, Bon Ami powder or Lava soap usually will do the job satisfactorily.

Hard as it is, the plastic surface can become badly scratched when used for cutting vegetables and other foods. Use a plastic or wooden cutting board instead.

Polishing Wheels: Very useful for hobby work and to keep home furnishings and equipment in top shape. An electric polishing and grinding outfit may range from the miniature hand-held Dremel motor kit with various small burrs, stones, cutters and polishers, to a bench-mounted dual-wheel unit for brushing, buffing, sharpening and grinding. There are also grinding and buffing attachments as electric drill accessories, which can be used as a portable unit.

Wire-brush wheels spin off rust and paint. Carborundum wheels sharpen knives and chisels. Sanding discs, backed by a flexible rubber plate, cut through paint on car fenders and on wooden items. Polishing is done with a soft felt disc or cloth flaps, while soft cloth wheels do the final buffing on metals with the aid of a lime rouge in a dozen grades, from coarse to very fine—the finishing step in polishing.

Brushing and vacuuming after each use are necessary to pick up metal chips and sanding grit.

Pongee: A type of silk with a rough texture. After washing in mild detergent and lukewarm water, dry quickly with a fan to prevent watermarks. Press only when dry or almost dry, ironing on the wrong side to minimize wrinkling and scorching. (See *Silk,* page 152.)

Porcelains: There's hardly a home that does not have some prized procelains, perhaps just one or two delicately tinted figurines, rare chinaware, a Derby plaque or treasured bric-a-brac. Careful handling and proper cleaning can avoid damage while keeping these pieces gleaming.

A small artist's brush is necessary for reaching into recessed and contoured areas of figurines without the stress that results in breakage. Badger or similar springy bristles ½- to ¾-inch long, are preferred; camel's hair and sable brushes may be too soft. The procedure for washing figurines applies also to chinaware and other delicate and brittle porcelain items. Dip the pieces, one at a time, into a deep plastic pan partly filled with warm water and dish detergent. Allow each piece to soak for a minute or two, then remove and shake off excess water. Wipe with a soft paper towel. Check for gummy deposits and other blemishes. Most caked soil will yield to either alcohol or nail polish remover, applied with the tiny brush and wiped with a cotton swab or Q-Tip. Remnants of old repairs, usually done with cellulose type cement, can be peeled off in strips. Other glues can be dissolved in hot water, turpentine, alcohol or acetone—you may have to try each to find the correct one, and patiently allow sufficient time for the solvent to work. In any case, do not try to remove the glue by sanding, as that will affect the glaze.

Porcelain Cookware: See *Cookware,* page 57.

Porcelain Enamel: The traditional finish for major home appliances, such as the range and dishwasher, was for years a glass-smooth porcelain enamel, resulting from several coats of silicone glaze fired onto the steel sheeting at very high temperature. Cleaning such surfaces rarely requires more than a once-over with a damp cloth. The appliance finishes now are mostly baked-on synthetic enamel with an attractive high gloss that is nearly as durable and stain-resistant as porcelain and has certain desirable characteristics such as ease of color matching. It is difficult to distinguish between the two types of finishes, but the synthetic enamel is more susceptible to abrasion. Hence scrubbing it with a coarse soap pad can remove some of the coating; this is unlikely with porcelain. However, the damaged spot can be repaired by spraying with the matching enamel from an aerosol can. Indeed, the color of an entire appliance can be changed as desired by spraying, but the new coating will not be as stain-resistant or durable.

Pressure Cooker: See *Cookware,* page 62.

Pumice: A white abrasive powder produced by grinding volcanic lava. The most common grades for household purposes are FF and FFF, and fine to coarse (0 to 4/0). Use with water or oil for lubrication. Pumice is widely used for grinding and polishing surfaces.

Pyrex Ovenware: See *Cookware,* page 61.

Qiana: One of the nylon fibers developed by DuPont, Qiana has unique properties—elegant appearance, washability and excellent resistance to wrinkling. Qiana is widely used in tricot knits for intimate apparel.

Quilts, Comforters: Machine washing is practical for comforters with synthetic polyester fillers and nylon or rayon shells. Size may be the determining factor—can it be fitted into the machine without crowding?

Use a mild detergent (All has proved to be of exceptional value in restoring old and very delicate quilts). Add ½ cup of borax for water softening, set the dial for warm water. Transfer after the spin to a preheated dryer, set for the lowest temperature. For drying outdoors, place the quilt across two parallel lines 2 or 3 feet apart, but not in direct sunlight. As drying proceeds, fluff up the filler fiber to keep it from becoming solidly matted.

DOWN QUILTS: Cleaning down quilts and down-padded garments causes needless concern. The feathers, so soft and cuddly, are plenty durable, take to water like a duck. The nylon covering also can withstand many washings. The feathers when dry become fluffed up again like new. The vulnerable part is the quilt stitching that keeps the down from shifting and leaving sparsely filled spaces. Tumble drying takes care of a major part of the process.

Down quilts also may be dry-cleaned, of course, and some are labeled "dry clean only." If that is done, make sure that your quilt will be cleaned only with a fresh solvent.

The bathtub is a good place to launder a quilt or sleeping bag. Fill the tub about one-third full with lukewarm water (100 degrees); add a mild detergent like Joy, Chiffon or Lux. Toss in the quilt, let it soak for a while, then knead it so the solution swishes through the down for a good washing. Rinse with at least three changes of water, pressing but never twisting the quilt, to squeeze out as much water as possible each time.

Hang it on a line or bar over the tub for an hour or so; dripping water will lighten the quilt. Preheat the dryer for a few minutes, then set it for the lowest temperature and pop in the quilt. Include a pair of clean canvas sneakers, which will fluff up the down as the tub turns. Drying takes quite a long time, 3 or more hours, so be patient. Your quilt will come out sparklingly fresh.

Radiators: See *Steam Radiators,* page 170.

Radiator Air Valves: These valves release air in the radiator so that steam can enter. The valves then close automatically to prevent steam from escaping into the room. Grease or rust in the valve prevents function. Clean the valve by soaking it overnight in a tray of household vinegar to loosen rust. Replacement with a new valve is advisable since they are not too expensive and last many years. A valve that has been dropped or damaged in any way should be replaced, as repair is not practical. Caution: Never leave a radiator without its air valve, even for a short time. Have the replacement ready before removing the old one. Steam escaping into a room in volume will cause serious damage and may be lethal.

Ranges: The exterior surface of most ranges consists of baked-on porcelain enamel that is about as hard, smooth and glossy as glass. Do not confuse porcelain with ordinary enamel coatings—porcelain, more durable and attractive, needs just a swipe with a soapy sponge to keep it sparklingly clean. Daily washing and attention to preservation of the fine original finish will keep your stove looking brand new for years and years.

The surface porcelain, hard as it is, is vulnerable to certain influences: a heavy object dropped on the stove can chip the procelain, any touch-up repair will look patchy and eventually rub off; a sudden change of temperature by placement of a hot pan can crack or craze the surface coating; dragging pots or other rough metal over the enamel will ruin its gloss.

Spilled acidic foods, such as tomato and citrus juices, can also affect the porcelain. Special mats of the right width to fit stovetop areas have aluminum tops to dissipate heat from pots, and heat-resistant rubber bases (Rubbermaid Stove

Mat). Raised rims trap spillovers. Clean these mats with liquid detergent, do not use scouring powders.

EXTERIOR CLEANING: Wipe the entire surface, including the top control panel, with a soapy sponge or cloth; do not use abrasive scouring powders or steel wool. Clean stubborn spots with a plastic pad and liquid detergent. If necessary, remove caked-on substances with a mildly abrasive cleanser (Bon Ami, Ajax). Pull off the control knobs, wipe clean and replace. Do not soak knobs.

Stainless steel range cabinets are less vulnerable to damage and easier to keep clean—just with a wipe of a damp cloth in most cases, but make it a habit to wipe the range dry with a paper towel to avoid streaks and water spots.

STOVE TOP CLEANING (ELECTRIC): Make certain that all burner switches are turned off, units cool enough to handle. The burner coils never need cleaning because any spilled foods are burned off when the units are heated, but the coils must be removed for access to the drip pans underneath; these must be washed frequently. Remove the burner coils by lifting the edge opposite to the point where the electrodes are plugged in, pull back so the coil comes out. The drip pans now can be lifted out. Soak the drip pans in detergent solution or place in dishwasher.

The bright surface of the drip pans is necessary to reflect heat upwards onto the cookware. Do not use abrasive cleaners that could scratch or rub away the chrome coating, exposing the steel underneath to rusting. Aluminum foil liners for metal drip pans, purchased inexpensively at supermarkets, can eliminate the problem of spillovers. When using the liners on electric ranges, line up the side openings to clear the burner electrodes.

Ceramic-porcelain drip bowls can be placed in a self-cleaning oven, upside down on the oven racks, to be cleaned automatically when the oven is heat-cleaned.

Before replacing the drip pans and burner coils, lift the range top on its hinges and wipe clean the catch pan underneath.

STOVE TOP CLEANING (GAS): Remove the grates, soak in a pan with detergent solution or put into the dishwasher. Lift out each burner by pulling the tubular end out of the gas port. Soak the burners in a pan with detergent solution, clear any clogged holes in the burner ring with a fine wire or hairpin, but not a toothpick, which might break off. Shake out the water and replace, making sure each burner goes into its correct position. Avoid altering the air shutter in the burners.

If the stove has a hinged lid, raise it before replacing the burners and wash the catch pan underneath. If the pilot light has gone off, relight it with a match.

CERAMIC COOKING PANEL: Correct cooking and cleaning methods help keep a ceramic stove top (Corningware) looking like new with minimum fuss.

1. Keep cooktop always clean and dry. Do not use it if it is cracked.

2. Select correct heat settings and utensils of adequate size to eliminate spillovers and spatterings. If necessary, lower the heat.

3. Wipe up food spills and spatterings promptly, but don't use a wet sponge on a hot panel.

4. Clean the Corning cooktop after each use just as you do dishes. Use liquid dish detergent and plastic pads. Never use scouring pads or powders on the ceramic panel. Remove spillovers of sugar and syrups as quickly as possible, as they can damage the protective surface.

CLEANING THE STANDARD OVEN: For those who still have standard ovens without the new carefree coating, best policy is to tackle the job right off—while the oven is still warm, the grease not yet congealed. Lift off the door (if it is removable) for separate cleaning at the sink, to permit easier access to the oven interior and for removal of the shelves and broiler pan.

Use a sponge, the largest you have, with a liquid detergent; wipe soft grease off all interior surfaces—walls, top and bottom, and back panel. (If you have a gas oven, be careful around the pilot light and the thin gas tubing at the rear.) Go over the surfaces a second time to be sure all grease has been removed. Any spot that remains of scorched or spillover food tackle with a plastic soap pad (Rescue, Chore Girl), rubbing until it has been entirely removed.

If the cleaning can't be done at once, leave a bowl of diluted ammonia in the oven; it will soften the grease enough to make the job easier when you can tackle it. Caution: Do not use ammonia on aluminum pans.

Most commercial cleaners are extremely caustic, containing lye and nitrogen compounds. The cleaner is sprayed from aerosol cans over the entire oven interior, left on for several hours or overnight with the door closed. Wear rubber gloves and cover the floor nearby with newspapers; also watch that the caustic spray does not touch nearby painted surfaces; most important, open the windows for ventilation and avoid inhaling the spray. There are noncaustic, nontoxic cleaners (such as Arm and Hammer Oven Cleaner) which you may find as effective as the others.

Wash the broiler pan, shelves and the door if it has been removed at the sink with a nylon scrubbing pad. Parts that are small enough can go into the dishwasher. The softened grease in the oven is wiped off with a soapy sponge, but any remaining stubborn spots must be rubbed off patiently. A silicone spray (Oven Guard, Devcon, Fuller) inhibits buildup of carbonized grease in the oven.

If you have extinguished the pilot light, the way to start it again is to hold a lighted match under the automatic control nearby to heat it so that it opens and lets the gas through. Use a candle if you can't hold the match long enough.

The most useful recent improvement in ovens is the self-cleaning and continuous-cleaning systems, which eliminate one of the most arduous tasks in the home—that of washing up splattered grease and spillover foods in the oven. The new system uses heat to burn off grease and to disintegrate carbonized spots.

SELF-CLEANING OVEN: Close the oven door, set the dial as indicated on the control panel. A safety latch prevents opening the door while the 850- to 1,000-degree heat reduces grease and food spills in the oven to a fine ash that is easily wiped up with a sponge, leaving the oven interior and shelves in brand new condition. After a 2-hour heating period and the cooldown time, the current automatically shuts off and the safety door latch is released. A bell can be set to ring at that time. The cleanup is done at weekly or monthly intervals, as needed, and the oven is sufficiently insulated so that the intense heat is not transmitted to the room. Some models have in addition a protective shutter that comes up between the outer and inner door glass panels during the cleaning process. The self-cleaning and continuous-cleaning ovens are both available in gas and electric models.

The self-cleaning oven works on a pyrolytic principle, based on a catalyst and a new type of porcelain coating with an uneven, pebble-like surface. A grease splatter, instead of forming a solid drop on a smooth surface, spreads out and is partially absorbed by the special porcelain surface, and under the intense heat of the cleaning process is disintegrated.

An example is given by Whirlpool to explain the process: A drop of water on a waxed paper beads up into a large blob. But the drop of water on a paper towel spreads out and is absorbed. The porcelain is treated to follow a similar process.

CONTINUOUS-CLEANING OVEN: The cleaning action is the result of the specially treated porcelain enamel coating which causes fat and grease spatters to diffuse and gradually become reduced to ash as the oven is heated during normal baking and broiling. Never use a caustic or abrasive cleaner on the porcelain as it will affect its catalytic properties.

The continuous cleaning does not apply to noncoated parts such as the oven door and racks. Clean these when needed with soap-filled pads. A sheet of heavy-duty aluminum foil placed on the bottom shelf as a liner catches spills, which are often very difficult to wash away. Cut a half dozen or so sheets of foil to fit, stack them on the bottom shelf of the oven. Thus, when the top sheet becomes soiled and is discarded, the sheet of foil underneath takes its place.

MICROWAVE OVENS: Wipe up spills around the door seal, door surface or oven frame if they occur. Keep the filter free of soil and grease. Make sure the filter is in place before operating the oven. Use only cooking utensils recommended for the microwave oven, including glass, wood, paper or plastic—not metal.

SPILLOVERS: Fit a sheet of heavy-duty aluminum foil onto the oven pan below the broiler rack, the foil overlapping the pan a couple of inches at sides and rear so that the edges can be turned up to retain dripping grease, but allow some clear space to permit air circulation.

OVEN FLARE-UP: Keep an open box of baking soda handy in the kitchen to extinguish oven fires. Throw the soda directly onto the flames to smother them. Never attempt to put out a grease or electrical fire with water.

LIGHT BULBS: Replace a burned-out oven interior bulb only with a special 40-watt appliance bulb which is designed to withstand oven temperatures. Have a replacement bulb ready; pull the electric cord before turning out the old bulb—never leave an empty bulb socket. The bulb in self-cleaning ovens usually is shielded for safety. (See *Light Bulbs: Appliance,* page 104.)

OVEN DOOR GLASS: Clean the decorative glass panel with liquid dish detergent and warm water. Rinse and dry thoroughly to avoid streaks.

The brushed chrome trim on some oven doors can be polished with a paste made of baking soda or Bon Ami cleaner, rubbed on with a soft cloth pad, then rinsed and wiped with a fresh cloth to remove traces of the cleaner.

Rayon: An absorbent filament that loses strength when wet, rayon is often combined with other fibers in permanent-press blends used in making women's garments, draperies and upholstery fabrics. Rayon has been used with varying success for carpeting, tires and some industrial products.

Unless dry cleaning of garments is required to retain

shape and body, machine or hand wash in warm water with gentle agitation.

Refrigerator: Complete cleaning of the interior weekly keeps the refrigerator sanitary and free of odors. Turn the control knob to OFF or pull the electric plug, take out all food, remove racks, shelves, crisper baskets. Sponge the interior walls with a solution of 2 tablespoons baking soda or borax in 1 quart of warm water. Wipe the door gasket with a sudsy sponge, rinse and wipe dry. Do not use bleaches or petroleum-base cleaners on the door gasket. Wash the trays and racks separately with detergent. Refill ice trays with fresh water, and reset the refrigerator temperature control.

The trays and racks may be held in place by intricate retainer lugs; do not force them out. Rather, see the manufacturer's booklet for cleaning instructions if necessary.

For efficient operation, clear dust off condenser coils, which may be at the back or bottom, with the vacuum cleaner nozzle. Manufacturers advise against waxing of the exterior porcelain enamel.

Keep a cup of charcoal or an open carton of baking soda in a rear corner of the refrigerator for freshness.

Common portland cement also effectively prevents food odors. Make a paste with a cupful each of portland cement and vermiculite (mineral aggregate), ¼ cup of silica gel and ¼ cup of powdered chalk, moistened just enough for a thick paste. Harden in separate cans, dry in an oven at 300 degrees. Place a can at the back of a refrigerator shelf and change every few weeks, drying out the used can in the oven. Be sure to identify the contents of each can with a label.

Roof Gutters: Remove compacted leaves and other debris from the collectors and downspouts to assure rapid water runoff. Frequency of this cleaning depends on the leaf-shedding seasons and proximity of trees. Large-mesh plastic or aluminum screens installed over the gutters help prevent leaf accumulations, but an occasional cleanout still is advisable because sediment accumulates and slows water runoff. A garden cultivator is a good tool for the purpose; do not reach into the gutters with your bare hand.

Gutters on a one-story home are easy to reach; on taller houses, it may be best to leave the task to a handyman if you're not comfortable working on long ladders. While you're at it, run water from the garden hose into the gutters to check that they are properly pitched into the downspout openings, and see that the mounting straps provide sufficient support. If the downspout is not connected into the drainage system, see that a concrete splash apron is placed underneath the downspout outlet so rain water won't wear away the soil and leave stagnant puddles.

Rope (hawsers, halyards): Boat owners wouldn't think of mooring their boats until they have been washed down properly, but they may neglect care of the ropes, a valuable and essential piece of equipment. Keep ropes clean by washing with a mild detergent in fresh water to remove salt and dirt, which are abrasive and can cause rapid deterioration. Long rope may be washed while coiled by flushing with pailfuls of detergent and water. Another way to do this is to fill a large bucket with detergent in warm or hot water and slowly run the looped rope through its entire length.

Keep a second bucket handy, nearly full with clear water; run the rope through for rinsing in the same way. Three rinses in fresh water or hosing down the coiled rope leaves it fresh and new looking.

Occasionally stretch ropes out on the dock, remove twists and kinks, check for cuts, torn strands, and loosened splices. When not in use, store rope in a clean, covered area, out of the sun and rain.

Rottenstone: An abrasive powder used for polishing. Rottenstone, produced from limestone, is softer and finer than pumice, making it suitable for polishing metals, marble and other smooth surfaces. Available at crafts-supply stores.

Rubber Cement: Patches of rubber cement are frequently left on surfaces after pulling off masking tape, address labels, bandages and similar "self-adhesive" materials. The solvent for rubber cement is acetone, often referred to as "lacquer thinner," which is sold in art-supply and office-supply stores, and is also generally available in the home as nail polish remover.

Caution: Acetone is highly flammable. Apply the thinner directly to the surface, to dissolve the adhesive, then wipe clear with a cloth.

Small areas of the dry rubber cement may be removed quickly by rubbing with the fingers to form blobs of the cement, which can then be brushed away. Artists use a gutta-percha eraser to pick up dried rubber cement from drawings and layouts.

Rugs: See *Carpets and Rugs,* page 50.

Rust: Oxidation (rusting) of ferrous metals (iron, steel) occurs in the presence of moisture. A coat of paint prevents rust; touch up any damaged spots, particularly on the car body, promptly. You can buy a small jar or spray can of enamel to match your car color. Polished metal implements like chisels and plane blades should be kept in sealed envelopes or coated with oil if the storage area tends to become damp and threatens rusting.

Chemicals and abrasives are used for dealing with rust. One type of chemical, a gel sold in hardware stores as "naval jelly," dissolves the rust, which is flushed away with water. Another breaks down rust so that it dries and hardens into a smooth protective base like a primer coating, which can be painted. Abrasive treatment is done with sandpaper, wire brushes, steel wool, emery cloth or files. Mechanical removal can be done with sanding disks, backed by rubber pads in a portable drill. Similarly, small wire brushes in hand-held drills (Dremel Handy Kit) will clean small rusted areas. Another tool is the flap wheel, consisting of closely packed strips of abrasive paper mounted on a circular hub which is chucked into the drill.

When using a chemical gel such as naval jelly, coat the rusted parts and allow to stand for at least 24 hours, then wash with warm water—repeat the process if necessary. Rust problems often occur on auto bodies, outdoor hand railings, and iron patio furniture. Complete removal of the rust down to the bare metal is desirable, but this often cannot be accomplished because of deep pitting. Small areas of chipped paint on autos should be touched up with matching paint, as mentioned above, before rust sets in.

For stoop railings, patio furniture, roof gutters and downspouts, a coating of Rust-Oleum paint is the simplest answer; it inhibits further oxidation and provides a finish coating.

RUST STAINS ON PORCELAIN BATHTUBS AND SINKS: See *Bathtubs,* page 40; *Sinks and Bathtubs,* page 155.

Safety at Home

BURNS AND SCALDS: Place kettles and pans securely on the range when cooking; turn spout of kettle so steam from boiling water is not in your direction. Use deep enough saucepan when deep-fat frying.

ELECTRICITY: It's truly a marvel that this powerful force can be utilized safely even by a child, switching on the lights or the TV. But electricity can indeed be dangerous, even lethal, if normal good practices are neglected. The following rules provide the basics for electrical safety in the home:

1. Avoid touching a faucet, pipe, sink, radiator or other conductive surface while handling or plugging in an electrical appliance.

2. See that every appliance you buy has the Underwriters Laboratories (UL) label.

3. Never keep a plugged-in radio, shaver, hair dryer or other electrical equipment within reach of the bathtub. Do not use any electrical device when your hands are wet or while you are standing on a damp floor.

4. Do not immerse any electric appliance in water unless

it is specifically designated as safe. If an electric shaver drops into a water-filled sink, pull the plug immediately; do not use it again until inspected by a competent serviceman.

5. If an appliance has a cord with connecting devices at both ends, plug into the appliance first before inserting the other end into the line receptacle. This helps avoid sparks and burns. Reverse this when disconnecting—pull out the wall receptacle plug first.

6. Keep a bulb in every lamp socket. When removing the base of a broken bulb, pull the cord plug first, if the current was turned on when the bulb failed, or disconnect the fuse or circuit breaker.

Newer tools and some appliances have 3-prong grounding cords to be used in safety wall receptacles that take the round extra prong. The purpose is that if the tool's casing becomes charged with current, the electricity will flow harmlessly through the ground wire. If your wall receptacles are not of this modern safety type, it is worthwhile to change them. Failing this, an adapter socket can be used and grounded to the center screw in the outlet plate.

Do not remove the grounding cord from a washing machine or other stationary appliance; do not use any equipment if the ground wires are disconnected or missing.

Don't use an electric tool such as a drill or hedge clipper outdoors on a wet day or in a damp environment. Any extension cord used outdoors must be of the 3-wire, grounded type, the wire of sufficient thickness (gauge) in proportion to the length of the cord.

FIRES: Teach children fire safety; rehearse the family in several fire emergency exits, following a plan. Keep careful control over all matches in the home; store them in capped glass or metal containers.

FLAMMABLE LIQUIDS: Keep all flammable liquids in metal or plastic containers, rather than glass, and store only small quantities indoors, on a shelf or in a well-ventilated cupboard.

GAS RANGE: Use only for cooking, not for heating. Make certain there's adequate ventilation whenever the flame is on.

ELECTRIC RANGE: Don't touch an electric heating coil before ma
ing sure it is cool. Remember the coil retains heat for son
time after the current is shut off.

GLASS: Do not keep glass bottles or jars in the shower stall,
around the edge of the bathtub. Wherever possible, transf
contents to plastic containers, which won't shatter if droppe
into the tub or on a tile floor.

If you have sliding glass patio doors, put on decals so th
glass is readily visible; remove any small rugs nearby tha
might slide under anyone or cause anyone to trip.

HAMMERS: One of the most familiar household tools can also b
one of the most hazardous. Wear safety goggles when usin
any striking tool, to protect eyes from flying metal or ma
sonry chips. Discard any hammer whose head shows ev
dence of chipping or spalling. Replace loose or cracked han
mer handles.

LAWN MOWERS: When using a power mower, keep children ou
of the way; rake the lawn first to remove loose stones an
other debris that could be tossed into the air by the mowe
blades. Wear sturdy shoes; never go barefoot. Shut down th
engine before clearing the discharge port or making an
adjustments. Store gasoline supply outside the home in a
approved metal can. Allow the mower engine to cool befor
refilling the tank.

MEDICINES: Keep all medicines in original containers, labeled, i
a safe place. Have ample light on the medicine cabinet t
prevent mixing up medications. Request safety caps on pre
scription containers, if there are children in the house.

POISONS: Keep an antidote chart pasted onto a medicine cabine
door for fast reference, together with the telephone number
of your doctor and hospital. Of course, keep all poisonou
chemicals out of harm's way.

SNOW AND ICE: Anticipate hazards. Install railings, hand grips o
other supports where they are likely to help prevent fall:
Keep a supply of coarse salt handy for use on iced steps, als
a sack or pail of sand.

Saw Blades: Two deficiencies affect handsaws—they become coated with resin from wood during cutting, and the polished steel quickly becomes rusted when subjected to moisture, even from hand contact. Both resin and rust retard movement of the blade inside the wood kerf. Fortunately, only slight attention will overcome these problems. Rusting may be prevented by keeping the saw blade coated with oil when it's not in use—any light lubricating oil will do, wiped on with a cloth pad. When the saw is to be used, just wipe with turps or other mineral solvent so that the saw does not stick. Of course, you'll have to wipe on a new oil coating after you're through. Rustproof protection is obtained by storing the saw in a dampproof bag.

CIRCULAR SAW BLADES: These blades used in portable and stationary power tools usually are chrome-finished or of an alloy that resists rust, but the blades are likely to become sticky with wood gums after use. Wipe with any mineral solvent or vinegar; dry thoroughly.

Sawdust: When allowed to accumulate in the basement workshop, or elsewhere in the home, sawdust can cause accidents by making the floor slippery, create a musty odor by absorbing moisture from the air, and at the very least, make a room untidy. It is also a fire and explosion hazard.

Set aside special receptacles, preferably metal boxes or cans with tight covers, to receive the sawdust as it is produced when sawing wood. Bench saws have an opening behind the blade where a carton, placed inside the saw stand, catches the sawdust as it falls below. An optional attachment to radial saws has a large-diameter tube through which the sawdust is blown into a receiving box.

Dispose of sawdust promptly to remove a fire hazard. Use the crevice tool of the vacuum cleaner to pick up sawdust and wood chips behind doors, panels, and similar hiding places.

Sawdust, known also as "wood flour," is used when sweeping wet or dusty floors, and it is the chief component of an excellent hand cleaner that you make yourself, adding 1

ounce each of trisodium phosphate (TSP) and borax to 8 ounces of powdered soap. Mix the ingredients, combine with an equal quantity of fine "wood flour." The sawdust provides the gentle friction that promotes better cleaning. Powdered soap, by the way, is plain soap and not to be confused with "soap powder," which includes various other ingredients.

Screens: Whether in a door or window, a torn screen requires immediate repair. No ugly strip patching—you can put in a full new screen at very low cost if you do it yourself. The screen is held in place by a spline—a heavy cord or thin dowel pressed into a groove along the perimeter of the screen frame. Pull out the retaining spline, buy the required length of screen at your hardware dealer. You'll also need a screening tool having two small wheels, one concave and one convex.

The installation is easier if you take down the screen frame and place it flat on the floor. Arrange the new screening over the opening. With the wheeled tool, press two adjacent sides of the screening into the grooves. Then pull the screen fairly taut while the two other sides are set in place—not too tight, though, as spline pressure into the grooves will pick up any slack. Trim the excess screening that projects beyond the grooves with a razor blade after pressing in the spline cord all around.

Septic Tanks: One-third of all households in the United States depend on septic tanks and cesspools for sanitary disposal. Periodic cleaning of a septic tank at 3- to 5-year intervals, in most homes, is necessary to prevent overloading and blockage that can create messy and health-threatening conditions. Every new system should be checked after the first year of operation for sludge accumulation so the cleaning intervals can be more accurately scheduled.

Sludge depth is determined by lowering a measuring stick through the outlet pipe to the bottom of the tank; cleaning need not be done until the sludge level has risen to within 8 or 10 inches of the outlet pipe, or a total of about 2½ feet. Cleaning is done by commercial firms equipped with tank trucks fitted with pumps. Negotiate a total price beforehand to be sure of no unexpected charges. There is no need for hosing down or flushing the tank, a service the tank operators often promote, nor are the various chemical additives, yeasts, bacteria and enzymes considered to be of any value in improving the functioning of the sanitary system, and certainly they do not lessen the need for occasional emptying.

The sludge accumulation determination can be useful also in indicating the extent of the family's water consumption and perhaps provide an incentive for avoiding wasteful use of water. The government manual on septic tanks, listed in Part III in the booklet section, may be helpful.

Shades: See *Window Shades,* page 183.

Sharpening: Knives and other cutting tools become dulled when the very thin metal on the blade edge "folds over," forming a rough burr. Sharpening removes this burr, restores the smooth and keen bevel, which will give you safer, effortless slicing.

Sharpening is done by stroking the knife blade back and forth across a carborundum "stone" or a tempered steel rod. The most convenient type is a small "stone" with a wooden handle for easy gripping (Stanley Kitchen Sharpener No. 66). Plane blades and chisels are sharpened by drawing the bevel edge along a rectangular-shaped silicon carbide stone.

Keep your knives in a wooden rack with individual slots so that they do not touch. Tossing knives into drawers with other metal objects will surely cause nicks that require regrinding, a needless and expensive process that narrows the blade and alters the temper of the steel.

Kitchen and pocket knives are sharpened by drawing the cutting edge foremost against the stone surface, in either a straight or circular motion. Just a few strokes on each side of the bevel usually suffice. Do not try to sharpen knives with a serrated or wavy edge, as these require special equipment.

WHETSTONES: Apply a light lubricating oil to keep the sharpening stone, called a whetstone, in good condition. The oil floats away metal grit and abrasive dust, preventing the stone's surface from becoming glazed and thus impairing its cutting power. After each use, wipe away the old oil, as it may be gritty. Apply a new coating of oil to the stone before storing it.

Clean the stone occasionally with a stiff-fiber brush and kerosene or lighter fluid. If this does not produce the required result, rub the stone face down on a piece of coarse abrasive paper that is tacked onto a truly flat surface, then re-oil for storage.

Shipping Labels: Protect the address from smearing, particularly if it has been written with water-soluble felt-pen ink, by covering the writing with strips of transparent cellulose tape of the nonreflective type. Another way is to rub over the address lightly with a candle, which gives it a protective waxed surface. When applying self-adhesive labels, run the edge of your palm across to obtain secure adhesion.

Shoes: Frequent polishing preserves leather shoes and boots from the drying effects of mud and water. The oil and wax in paste polish keeps the leather pliable and dampproof; the smooth finish helps prevent scuffing. Apply the polish with a cloth pad or suedelike applicator, rubbing the paste into the sole seam and onto the tongue cover, then brush vigorously over the entire surface to produce a glistening polish. Let shoes rest at least a day or two between wearings; store them with shoe trees so they keep their shape while drying out.

Hiking boots and children's shoes are waterproofed by rubbing on saddle soap or spraying on a lanolin-based compound. Leather soles will be long lasting, always pliable, when treated with one or two applications of neat's-foot oil or saddle soap—excellent also for removing squeaks from new shoes. Shoes subject to contact with portland cement and other alkaline substances should be kept well greased. Patent leather shoes will stay shiny if given an occasional light coating of castor oil, which also will help prevent cracking of the leather.

SNEAKERS—TENNIS SHOES: If muddy, allow to dry, then brush off. Remove spots with treatment for the particular stain. If only spots are mud or grease, wash sneakers like any garment.

White canvas shoes can be put into the washing machine with detergent and bleach. If a grease spot remains, use prewash concentrate and wash again; finish with a coat of whiting, a finely powdered form of calcium carbonate (chalk) in liquid form (Lano-White). This has a mildly abrasive action that helps clean the canvas while whitening it. Rubber soles can be cleaned by brushing with a heavy-duty detergent. (See also *Canvas Shoes,* page 50.)

Shower Curtains: Most plastic shower curtains can be laundered in the washing machine with warm water, but only for 3 to 5 minutes of agitator time. Fill the machine to capacity with water; avoid crowding. Use ½ cup detergent. After rinsing, remove before the spin cycle. Do not put the curtain into the dryer; rather, shake off excess water and wipe with terry towels; hang to dry. Bathroom curtains are particularly subject to mildew; allow to dry thoroughly, then spray with a disinfectant (Lysol, Listerine) to help prevent mildew.

Shower Nozzle: With time, the tiny holes in the shower head become clogged with sand or impurities and the water ceases to spray properly. Take down the shower head by turning the large nut that attaches it to the pipe. (You will need an open-end wrench or pliers; cover the fixture with bandage or masking tape to protect the chromed surface.) Reverse flush the clogging substance with a stream of water and replace the head. If water drips at the pipe joint, put in a new rubber washer similar to the type used for a garden hose. Draw the connector nut taut with moderate pressure; do not over-tighten. Adjust the position of the shower nozzle on its flexible ball joint as desired.

Showers: See *Stall Showers,* page 168.

Siding: See *House Siding,* page 93.

Silk: Luxuriously soft and smooth, silk fabrics also are quite strong and durable, but wrinkle easily. Dry cleaning is usually called for by the label and is essential for certain types such as taffetas, which lose crispness, and chiffon textiles, which tend to shrink when placed in water. Hand washing, however, is preferred by many homemakers for convenience, economy and to preserve the luster of the fabric. Before washing, test a piece snipped from a seam for colorfastness in water.

Use a white soap or a mild detergent; wash in lukewarm water (less than 100 degrees). Add a teaspoon of borax (Arm & Hammer) to soften the water. Remove belts, buckles and ornaments that might stain or rip the garment. Wash by squeezing the water through the material several times; rinse with at least three changes of fresh water.

Never use chlorine bleach on silks; sodium perborate powder is acceptable, though it is not fully effective at the mild water temperature.

A silk garment is dried by first rolling in a turkish towel to remove most of the water, then placed on a wooden or plastic hanger, which will help retain the garment's shape and avoid wrinkling. Any wrinkle that persists can be touched up with an iron set for low temperature. Do not dry silk near heaters or in the direct sunshine.

Silver: The gleam of a brightly polished silver service is the decorative highlight of many homes. For those who relish the eye-catching sheen of well-cared-for sterling, the regular weekly or monthly polishing session is considered recreational; others find that task a dreary chore and are quite pleased to accept alternate means of keeping the silver in condition.

Silver's affinity for sulfur compounds, which are always in the air, causes tarnishing. The chief function of silver polish is to remove this tarnish and the polishes that do the job most easily—and seemingly most brightly—are precisely those that are most abrasive, causing more wear and more scratches. A good compromise is a polish that is only slightly abrasive, therefore requiring a bit more effort but leaving the silver in its most lovely brilliance. One of the long-time and highly regarded silver polishes is Gorham, used around the world. Bon Ami in cake form, containing soap and feldspar, is somewhat softer than the silica of other cleaners and is quite effective for quick cleanup of tableware, but may cause discernible markings on larger surfaces like serving trays.

Silverplate calls for careful avoidance of harsh abrasives. Use only liquid metal polishes with a flannel cloth or felt for rubbing, never a scouring pad. Cleaning is aided considerably by boiling in mild vinegar or a solution of baking soda, then rubbing with facial tissue or cloth with a soft nap.

PREVENTING TARNISH: Use your silver as often as possible, reducing need for polishing. Furniture or floor wax will help prevent tarnishing, but at the expense of dulling the silver's glow. Plastic transparent bags, such as those used for wrapping foods, make good anti-tarnish storage containers. Cotton flannel cloths treated with zinc acetate also will preserve silver brightness, when tightly wrapped. Commercial wrapping cloths are available, as are the newer, instant cleaning liquids for dipping silver. Storing silver in metal containers, with the cover sealed airtight, will keep silver bright for a long period.

Electrolytic "no-rub" cleaning results when tableware is placed in an aluminum pan with a solution of 1 teaspoon of baking soda and one teaspoon TSP in a quart of boiling water. Each item of tableware must touch the aluminum pan. Allow to boil for 2 or 3 minutes, drain. (Wash the pan to avoid darkening the aluminum.)

SILVER REPLATING: A cherished tea service or an old silver bowl on which the plating has worn to the extent that the base metal, usually brass, shows through, can be replated to newlike condition. Deep scratches, even undesired monograms, are removed in the process. Replating is quite expensive, often exceeding the original cost of the article, so it would not be economical to have this work done unless the item is of unique design or valued as an antique or heirloom. A reliable silverplater may be difficult to find, as not many accept work on individual pieces. You would probably do best to turn over the job to your local jeweler who would have contact with these firms and know which meet adequate standards.

Properly replated silverware can be expected to retain its beautiful appearance for 20 years in normal service. Silversmiths advise that silver and silverplate be used often, even for everyday service, rather than saved for company dinner as is customary in many homes.

Sinks and Bathtubs

PORCELAIN: Most soil can be wiped up from porcelain sinks and bathtubs with a soapy sponge. Buff dry with a soft cloth to remove water spots. Avoid scouring powders. Clean mild stains and film around faucets by rubbing with baking soda. In hard-water areas, there may be a buildup of soap scum around the tub. A nonprecipitating water softener on a damp sponge will dissolve soap film. Try wiping stubborn coatings with vinegar.

Rust or blue mineral spots may yield to a solution of 1 part oxalic acid to 10 parts water. (Oxalic acid, purchased at paint supply stores, is poisonous. Wear protective goggles and gloves.) On a vertical surface under a faucet, mix the acid solution with cornmeal, making a thick paste, but do not let any of it get on chrome hardware. Let stand several hours, then rinse away.

For medicine stains on porcelain, use a paste made of cream of tartar and hydrogen peroxide. Allow the paste to remain until it dries into a powder, which is dusted away. Rubbing usually is not necessary. (See also *Bathtubs*, page 40; *Stains: Porcelain Fixtures*, page 165.

SINK RIMS: Food debris that accumulates along the inside edge of the metal molding around kitchen porcelain sinks may be difficult to remove. If the discoloration cannot be scored away with a narrow brush and soap, try scraping with the tip of a manicuring orange stick or similar soft wood article. Use of a sharply pointed tool such as a knife or awl is not advisable because of the possibility of digging out the putty that seals the sink rim to the countertop, leaving a space that will only result in further soil accumulation.

STAINLESS STEEL: Scratches can be smoothed with very fine steel wool, rubbed in a single direction with the grain. Buffing with a dry cloth removes watermarks and fingerprints. The best way to keep stainless steel always bright and clean is to wipe it dry after each use.

Skillet (Electric): Maintain the attractive appearance and cooking efficiency of the skillet by thorough cleaning after each use. Fats and salts allowed to remain in it for prolonged periods form a film that will cause discoloration when the skillet is reheated.

If immersible according to the manufacturer's instructions, let the skillet cool completely before placing it in a sink or automatic dishwasher, first detaching the heat control. The skillet may be cleaned in hot soapy water with a sponge or plastic pad. Do not use a metal scouring pad or harsh scouring powder or scrape dried-on foods with a knife. Dry promptly after rinsing to prevent water spots. Wipe heat control with a damp cloth.

Golden brown or blue heat tints that result from persistent overheating can be scrubbed away with a nonabrasive cleaner that does not contain chlorine bleach, rubbing lightly in a circular motion.

Skunk: See *Odors,* page 117.

Slate Flagstones: Bring up the color and brightness of slate flagstones by waxing or with an application of furniture polish, wiping away any excess that has not been absorbed by the stone. Mortar between patio and walkway stones is cleaned with detergent, moistened sawdust and a scouring brush. If an electric floor scrubber is used, move it continuously to avoid crumbling the mortar.

Stained flagstones usually respond to treatment with one of the various driveway-cleaner compounds, sold at hardware stores (Florco, Garage Magic, Gunk Swab). The liquid is spread on to draw the grease, then flushed away with the garden hose. Another way is to sprinkle dry portland cement over the stain, saturate with paint thinner and let stand for several hours. Dispose of the cement powder properly, so it won't soil the lawn or cling to your outdoor furniture.

Sleeping Bag: See *Quilts,* page 134.

Slicing Machine: After each use, dismantle the machine as far as possible, removing the circular blade for cleaning. Machines with a manual crank should be flushed with hot running water, then soaked in a detergent solution. Sanitize the parts by dipping in a strong bleach solution, rinse in clean water and dry with clean towels. Check carefully for any clinging food particles.

Electric machines can be partly taken apart; clean as above, particularly the circular blade, but do not immerse the motor section unless this is specifically approved by the manufacturer. (See also *Knives: Electric Knife,* page 97.)

Slow Cooker: Unplug cord from outlet, then wipe base with a damp cloth. Do not immerse the base in water. Clean the porcelain exterior finish with hot soapy water, using a sponge, dishcloth or nylon pad with a nonabrasive cleaner. Do not use steel wool or harsh scouring powders. Clean the acrylic interior with hot soapy water and a sponge or dishcloth.

To remove a stain inside the crock, try scouring with Bon Ami or with soap-filled scouring pads. An occasional thorough cleaning with Dip-It solution or a Teflon cleaner will keep the utensil in top condition.

Smoke Detectors: Accumulated dust and grime can "confuse" the detector, lead to false alarms or, still worse, failure to function in response to smoke or flame. Vacuum clean the area around the alarm periodically, reachi ıg with the extension tube of the cleaner. Do not touch the interior of the detector. Test the unit after each cleaning, pressing the test button to sound the buzzer. A more dependable test is to drift smoke (from a lighted cigarette or pipe) into the chamber. The unit should emit a loud, shrill sound. Some battery-powered detectors will sound a repeated "beep" signal to warn of battery failure. Batteries generally should be replaced at least once a year.

Spandex: A lightweight synthetic fiber with a high degree of elasticity—both stretch and recovery. This yarn is often blended with nylon for swimwear, foundation garments, stretch pants and surgical supports.

Spandex may be hand or machine washed, in lukewarm water. Some types may be bleached; others not. (Follow label directions.) Spandex fabric tends after extended exposure to the atmosphere to turn yellow. As the core of this synthetic filament is yellow, this discoloration usually cannot be changed by bleach, and thus is irreversible. (See *Elastic Garments,* page 72.)

Solvents: Paint thinners, alcohol, acetone and most mineral solvents are highly flammable. Exercise adequate caution in using and storing them in the home. Store in metal cans or plastic bottles with screw-on caps, plainly marked as to the contents. It's not safe to keep the solvents in glass containers that will shatter if dropped. Store them outdoors in the garage or toolhouse; limit the quantity kept in the home to a pint or so kept on an open shelf or in an adequately vented cabinet.

Varnolene is in the same petroleum molecular chain as kerosene, and approximately the same price range. Varnolene does not have the distinctive odor of kerosene that many find objectionable and is therefore preferred for home use.

Buy varnolene at paint supply and hardware dealers in quart or gallon containers. Varnolene is flammable but not explosive under ordinary conditions. Use it for cleaning up oil-paint spatters, degreasing auto parts, softening tar spots and similar purposes.

Stains

Prompt action before a stain "sets" makes it easier to remove the stain and helps prevent permanent damage. The longer it remains in the fabric, the harder it will be to get the stain out. The method for removing the stain will depend also on several factors: its type (whether greasy, nongreasy, or both), the fiber content of the fabric or characteristics of any other material involved, the fastness or stability of color, and even the location of the stain—whether it is in a prominent part of the garment or upholstery.

Stain removal at best is an iffy project. A spot-lifting solvent that is successful in one instance may be wholly destructive in another, spreading rather than lifting the stain, or causing colors to run.

GENERAL PROCEDURES: Soaking in cold water is the first emergency step, if the fabric seems to be washable. Sometimes the cause of the stain is not known, so any action taken would be guesswork; nevertheless, there are clues that let you identify it as one of three classes of stains: *greasy*—likely from gravy, butter, car grease; *nongreasy,* as from fruit juices, grass, or medicine like iodine; or a *combination* of both types, which may be chocolate or milk, for examples. There also is the effect of acid splatter—not really a stain but requiring similar and rapid treatment.

Several solvents used for stain treatment—benzene, kerosene, gasoline, acetone, turpentine—are extremely volatile and flammable. Others, like carbon tetrachloride, may be nonflammable but very toxic. Use either type outdoors if possible, always with adequate precautions: ample ventilation, no flame or smoking; avoid inhaling the fumes, wear rubber gloves if sensitive to the chemicals.

Solvent-type spot lifters and those containing perchloroethylene must not be used on rubber goods, leather, suede, most plastics, latex, acetates or varnished surfaces. Avoid spraying those solvents on electric wire insulation, or a rubber gasket such as on a refrigerator door.

ACID: Yellow or brown stains on colored fabrics caused by mild acids can sometimes be lightened by holding the stained part of the garment over a dish of household ammonia. Spilled sulfuric acid from a car battery eats through fabric unless the clothing is rinsed immediately with cold water and the acid neutralized as soon as possible with an ammonia solution.

ALCOHOL: The damage is not usually staining by the alcohol but rather "bleeding" of the colors in the fabric, a condition that cannot be reversed. Rapid rinsing in a cold-water solution with white vinegar can sometimes inhibit the alcohol action. For stains from alcoholic beverages, see the individual category.

Spots on carpet or upholstery also can be the running of the original yarn dyes rather than an external stain. Sponge up the alcohol spot quickly with a white vinegar solution to neutralize the alcohol, dry with paper towels.

BALL-POINT PEN (INK): No single solvent is effective for all ball-point inks, because of the varied ink formulas, so several different cleaners may have to be tried. Start with alcohol (rubbing alcohol will do); apply liberally and allow to soak in before blotting. If alcohol has no effect, try acetone (nail polish remover) but check first to make sure it doesn't affect the color of the fabric. If necessary, continue with one of the substitutes for carbon tetrachloride, either perchloro-ethylene (Renuzit) or a similar nonflammable stain remover.

BLOOD: Wash area with a solution of 1 teaspoon white vinegar in 1 quart of warm water, or place in an enzyme presoak; then spot with solvent-type cleaning fluid. Do not rub. Launder as usual. Persistent blood stains can be treated with diluted ammonia (but this should not be used for acetate fabrics). Peroxide also is helpful for removing the stains but can be used only where bleaching is not a problem.

BLUE SERGE: Remove shine by applying acetic acid (vinegar or lemon juice) with cheesecloth; allow to air-dry to remove odor. Press with steam iron.

BLUING: Soak a stain of excess bluing with a mixture of ½ tea-spoon of detergent and about an ounce of ammonia. Soak for about an hour, then launder in regular way. If stain persists, use a chlorine bleach on all fabrics except silk or wool, on which only peroxide should be used.

BRICKWORK: Splattered paint spots are very difficult to remove since the paint seeps into the masonry pores. Try several applications of a water-soluble paste-type paint remover, brushed on as thickly as possible and allowed to stand a cou-ple of hours. Then scrape off with a stiff-bristle or wire brush, and flush with the garden hose. Several applications of the paste may be required. Any light-colored residue of the paint can be hidden by rubbing the area with a piece of broken brick, or simply darken with lampblack, which will eventu-ally wash away leaving the paint almost invisible.

BUTTER OR MARGARINE: Scrape up any solids on surface with blunt edge of a knife. Apply a dry-cleaning solution, following method for *Greasy Stains* (below).

CANDLE WAX: Scrape off as much as you can, cover area with several layers of paper towels, press with warm iron until wax is absorbed.

CANDY: Usually easy to remove by sponging with plain water, but add a mild detergent in more stubborn cases. For candies with red dye, soak in strong laundry detergent with chlorine bleach.

CARROT JUICE: Stain usually comes out in laundering. If not, use a presoak detergent or try cleaning fluid.

CATSUP: Remove as soon as possible, flushing with concentrated detergent and water. Wash out remainder of stain with glycerine, scraping with a blunt knife, if necessary, to release solid matter.

CHEWING GUM: Harden the gum with ice cubes so it can be scraped with a dull knife. Then place fabric face down on paper towels and sponge with dry-cleaning fluid applied through the fabric. Change the paper towels as they absorb the dissolved gum.

On floor tiles, stairs, and similar hard surfaces, scrape off as much of the dried gum as possible; use a dry-cleaning fluid, then sandpaper as needed to remove the remainder.

CIGARETTE BURN: If material is only lightly charred, apply dry-cleaning solution; follow when dry with bleach. Burned spot on carpet usually can be cut away by clipping the blackened ends of the tufts. Serious burns on garments may have to be repaired by weaving. On solid surfaces, such as the plastic laminate sheeting on kitchen counters, the charred area can be cut away with a hole saw of required diameter, and a matching section glued in its place.

COFFEE: Soak quickly in detergent with oxygen bleach, using hottest water the fabric can stand. On white cotton, nylon, rayon and acetate, use chlorine bleach; on wool and silk, use perborate bleach. Treat coffee with cream as a greasy stain.

CRAYON MARKS: Most crayons have a wax base that can be dissolved with a mineral solvent such as benzene or turpentine. Crayon marks on wallpaper, when softened by the solvent, may soak in permanently and even spread the discoloration, so removal requires the blotting or lifting method applied as for greasy stains. Do this by dampening a wad of paper toweling or paper napkin with the solvent. Press the wad over the crayon stain to absorb the softened wax. Do not rub. Repeat the process with new paper wadding until the stain is reduced as much as possible. On white wall covering, it is possible to camouflage any remaining discoloration with whiting, which will eventually rub off but will lighten the spot.

EGG: Scrape the residue with dull edge of a knife; apply cold water and detergent for several minutes, flexing the material between the fingers; then wash in soap or detergent, brushing the stained area.

FRUIT JUICES: Flush area as soon as possible with warm water and detergent. Brown stains, due to sugar in the fruit, may not show up until the sugar dries. The stains then are difficult to remove, and practically impossible to remove on wool. Try a small amount of white vinegar, then launder again in hottest water.

GELATIN: Normal laundering in water not over 100 degrees will remove the stain.

GLUES: While still soft, remove as much glue as possible with knife edge, shampoo with commercial cleaner. Glues vary considerably in composition—refer to the original package for cleaning instructions. Many common glues may be softened with a few drops of nail polish remover.

GRASS: Alcohol will remove the green color, but first check to see that the alcohol will not cause the material dye to run. Flush with clear, cold water. A few drops of ammonia may help restore the original appearance.

GRAVY: Scrape up surface liquid, clean spot with mineral solvent; follow *Greasy Stain* method (below); let dry and vacuum.

GREASY STAINS: Scrape up any remaining solids with a flat knife. Place fabric so stain is face down on folded paper towels.

Pour some cleaning solvent through the fabric onto the stained area, rub with a clean white cloth outward from the center of the stain so the oil is absorbed by the paper toweling underneath. Change paper towels as needed. Finally, launder as usual.

On upholstery fabric, sponging the surface with white vinegar or a dry-cleaning solution may be the only effective method of stain removal. Limit the solvent to the immediate area of the stain; apply folded paper towels repeatedly to soak up the dissolved grease. Blot, do not rub. With velvet, a delicate material, stain removal is more difficult and complex, may cause permanent matting of the nap. Dampen a wad of cheesecloth with dry-cleaning fluid, place over the stain and tap gently to dissolve and transfer the staining grease to the cheesecloth. Let the velvet dry before stroking with a soft brush to restore the nap.

INK: Place cheesecloth or an old towel under the stained area; apply concentrated ammonia, worked in with toothbrush handle or similar blunt tool. The cheesecloth blotter will absorb the ink as it starts to run; then apply vinegar to neutralize the ammonia.

Permanent (indelible) ink used on documents and laundry markings is expected to last a long time. If spilled, chances are it can't be removed without damage to the fabric, unless thinned with turps or similar solvent and scrubbed out while still wet. Bleaching with chlorine or peroxide bleach is sometimes effective in reducing or lightening the ink stain. (See also *Ball Point Pens,* above.)

Washable-ink stains on colorfast material usually can be removed. First soak up as much of the ink as possible with a blotter, then put through a washing machine cycle. Rubbing alcohol may be effective on these stains.

For ink-stained fingers, rub with the sulphur end of a match or wash with 5 percent solution of potassium permanganate, available at drug stores. (See also *Furniture,* page 85.)

IODINE: Pat stain with cheesecloth moistened with photographer's hypo solution (sodium thiosulfate) as soon as possible; follow with a drop or two of ammonia, then rinse with cold water. Fresh iodine stains also are reduced by applying a cotton pad moistened with rubbing alcohol, but stain may spread. Exposure to sunshine also may be effective.

IRON RUST: See *Rust Stains on Fabrics,* page 166.

LATEX PAINT: While paint is still wet, flush or sponge with water, then launder or wash spotted area with soap and water. Dried paint usually can't be softened, but try rubbing the fabric together to grind the paint into powder. On woodwork, remove fresh paint with a wet sponge. If paint has dried, use a scraper and fine-grit sandpaper.

LEAD PENCIL: Work glycerine or strong detergent into the marking; apply a little ammonia, then flush away.

LIPSTICK: On fabrics, treat like greasy stain. Place stain side face-down on a pad of paper towel, apply dry-cleaning fluid through back of fabric, rubbed with a sponge. Change paper towel for fresh surface as needed. Launder washable fabrics.

On mirrors and metals, wipe off lipstick with cloth dampened with cleaning fluid, but do not do this on varnished furniture. Instead, try washing with sudsy cloth.

MERCUROCHROME: Easy to flush out of nylon and other synthetic fabrics, but most difficult to remove from wool. First try glycerine or a concentrated solution of detergent. As stain runs, soak up as much as possible with a towel placed underneath to absorb the stain. Wash with detergent and ammonia, then rinse. White fabrics may need bleaching.

MILDEW: If garment is washable, launder in soap or detergent, but watch effect on color before using chlorine bleach. Walls, furniture and other home areas can be scrubbed with a heavy-duty cleaner followed by a bleaching agent, or spray on a mildew remover with calcium hypochlorite. Leather goods, shoes and other garments should be exposed to direct sunshine and scrubbed to remove the mildew spores. In some cases, it will not be possible to salvage the mildewed garment. (See *Mildew,* page 112.)

MILK: Sponge the area with a detergent solution to which a few drops of ammonia have been added. Old stains may require soaking in an enzyme, purchased at drugstores. Milk stains that have become set often cannot be removed from resin-treated fabrics.

MUD: Allow to dry, then brush vigorously; sponge remainder with warm water. Laundering usually removes any further trace of the stain.

MUSTARD: Do not use soap. Work glycerine into the stain, flush with detergent solution. If stain remains, let a professional "spotter" at the dry cleaners have a crack at it, but don't blame him if he's not successful in removing the yellow stain.

NAIL POLISH: Dissolve in acetone (amyl acetate), commonly called nail polish remover. Do not use on rayon or acetates.

PAINT: Turpentine, benzene, most cleaning fluids are solvents for oil and acrylic paints. Fresh spatters on woodwork can be wiped up with a solvent-soaked cloth. On clothing, follow the method for greasy stains, turning the stain over on paper toweling, but there's the possibility the solvent will cause the fabric colors to run, or will spread the stain discoloration while removing most of the paint.

For dried paint on a hard surface, apply a paint remover (use the nonflammable water-wash type); allow to stand an hour or more, wash clean, then use a mineral solvent (varnolene, turpentine) to neutralize and clean the area. See *Latex Paint Stains,* above.

PERSPIRATION: Launder fresh stains with detergent or soap. For old stains, use detergent and vinegar. Color changes resulting from the acidity may be permanent, but try holding over ammonia fumes to restore the color.

PORCELAIN FIXTURES: Three types of stains are common on porcelain fixtures:

1. *Blue stain, caused by a dripping faucet.* Rub lightly with a plastic soap pad, then bleach discoloration with chlorine. If necessary, use a mild cleanser (Bon Ami, Ajax). Stop the drip

with a new faucet washer and, if necessary, a new washer seat.

2. *"Rust" stain, due to iron in the water; usually dark gray in color.* Try lemon juice and salt, or chlorine bleach, applied with a sponge. If that fails, rub with a paste of moistened TSP with chalk, or try an oxalic acid solution (poisonous)—one tablespoon of crystals to a cup of water—on a sponge, rubbing until the stain fades or disappears.

3. *Medicine stains from tincture of iodine, mercurochrome, Betadine or similar.* Mix a paste of hydrogen peroxide and cream of tartar, apply to surface and allow to remain until it dries to a powder. Dissolved photographic hypo crystals (sodium thiosufate), and moistened perborate laundry bleach also will be effective.

RED INK: Sponge with peroxide bleach, then flush with ammonia water to remove acid. Repeat if necessary.

RUBBER CEMENT: Allow residual or spilled cement to dry; rub with fingers to remove as much as possible. Brush away the blobs of dry cement. Labels on appliances and shipping containers often leave residual strips of rubber cement when peeled off. For larger areas, dissolve the cement with acetone (flammable) and wipe with a cloth, which should then be discarded safely.

RUST STAINS ON FABRICS: Wash in lemon juice and salt solution. Commercial rust removers contain hydrofluoric acid or oxalic acid, toxic chemicals which are hazardous for household use. Rinse thoroughly after stain vanishes. Chlorine or perborate bleach often is effective for rust-stain removal by oxidation.

SCORCHES: On furniture, plastic countertops and similar hard surfaces, sand the scorched area with fine-grit paper or fine steel wool to remove the charred ash, then bleach out any discoloration with chlorine or perborate laundry bleach. Use oxalic acid solution (caution: poisonous) if necessary on dark, charred areas; neutralize the acid with borax powder. Rinse and allow to dry thoroughly. To restore the natural oils of the wood, rub in linseed or a clear mineral oil; wipe off excess after a few minutes. Apply stain if needed to blend with original color, then restore the finish coating, whether of lacquer, varnish or rubbing oil. Hand rubbing with a cabinet polish and felt pad helps blend in the repaired section so that it is not obvious.

Burns on plastic laminates can be made less visible by light sanding. Most often, however, the scorch is beyond repair, and resurfacing with a new laminate sheet will be necessary, except for an inconspicuous spot where the damaged area can be cut out with a hole saw of sufficient diameter in an electric drill. The same hole saw is used to cut the round replacement from a spare piece of the plastic; the scorched piece is pried loose from its backing panel and the replacement circle put in with rubber cement. There will be a slight gap around the patch representing the width of the saw kerf, but the counter will be otherwise serviceable.

Fabrics usually are beyond salvage when heavily scorched, unless the burn is in an inconspicuous part of the material. The only recourse may be lightening the scorch with diluted chlorine or perborate bleach while laundering.

silk: Yellow discoloration sometimes can be lightened with concentrated vinegar or peroxide, applied lightly with a cloth pad. Water spots are particularly difficult to remove from neutral shades or white silk, but shine on a dark silk garment can be treated by sponging with vinegar or acetic acid.

sink: See *Stains: Porcelain Fixtures,* page 165; *Sinks and Bathtubs,* page 155; *Bathtubs,* page 40.

soot: Soak garment or affected area in Wisk or similar prewash solution after brushing briskly, then launder. Discoloration is likely to remain, but try bleaching.

tar: Soften with Vaseline or a grease, then wipe with carbon tetrachloride or Renuzit on a sponge or cloth.

tea: On textiles, first try washing with warm water and detergent. A residual discoloration may require bleaching, but be careful not to affect the color. Do not use chlorine bleach on silk, wool, elastics or foam padding like polyurethane. Some fabrics can take bleaching with sodium perborate or hydrogen peroxide, or simply exposure to strong sunlight. Tea stains on marble usually respond to concentrated chlorine bleach. Apply by pouring on a small quantity, allow it to stand for several minutes, then wash it off.

TOBACCO JUICE: Rub in glycerine, soak in detergent and warm water. Bleaching may be necessary. The tannic content makes removal of tobacco stain difficult.

TOMATO JUICE: See *Stains: Catsup* page 161.

URINE: Soak in enzyme cleaning product with a little ammonia added, then launder. Sponging with diluted vinegar or perborate bleach may help set or restore the original color.

WATER SPOTS: The hazy white ring left on waxed wood surfaces by a cold perspiring glass containing water or an alcoholic beverage usually can be removed. Try first rubbing in wax with a cloth or felt pad. If this doesn't work, use a fine (No. 000) steel wool with the wax. When the ring is gone, blend in the area by vigorous buffing. As a last resort, strip off all the old wax and resurface, this time using a better-grade paste that is more resistant to water stains.

Water spots on taffeta: Sizing in the fabric is affected—no home treatment will work. Let your dry cleaner have a try at it.

WINE: Apply cold water as quickly as possible, then sponge with glycerine and detergent, rinsing with warm (not hot) water. If discoloration remains, apply a few drops of ammonia with detergent. Use white vinegar if stain turns pink. Some wine stains just can't be removed but may be lightened if the fabric can withstand bleaching.

Stall Showers: Deposits of soap scum, body oils, and hard-water minerals build up on shower walls and require cleaning. For ceramic tile walls, spray on an all-purpose cleaner, allow to soak in several minutes. Wipe the walls with a sponge and scrub the floor with a brush. Hard-water scum can be removed with a solution of white vinegar and water. Kerosene also is effective for this purpose, but the odor may be objectionable. The shower area is particularly subject to mildew; spray occasionally with a mildew-inhibitor and disinfectant. If shower area has become mildewed, scrub with a fungicide (calcium hypochlorite) or ammonia. Rinse well. If discoloration remains after the treatment, use a chlorine or peroxide bleach.

Reduce the possibility of mildewing by keeping the shower curtains or door open for light and ventilation.

The caulking where shower wall and tub meet may separate or crumble because of settling of the tub. Keep this caulked seal in good condition, recement any loose tile, replace grout cement as necessary.

Static Electricity: Those annoying shocks that make you jump each time you touch a doorknob are static electrical sparks, generated by the friction of walking across the carpet, for example. The spark, sometimes almost an inch long, can be seen in the dark. Such static electricity also is the reason garments cling in the dryer, subborn lint resists brushing, and pet hair forms clumps on upholstered furniture.

The drier the air and cooler the room, the more likely there will be a static electrical charge. Some people are more susceptible than others, possibly due to varied skin moisture. One way to reduce or eliminate the negative charge is to maintain a higher moisture level in the air during the winter months. This can be accomplished with an electric humidifier. In homes with hot-air heating, a humidifier with an automatically filled water pan is combined with the furnace. The incidence of static charges is reduced when temperature is above 70 degrees.

Padding the doorknobs with a rubber or plastic cover also helps eliminate the shocks.

There are chemical treatments and sprays that eliminate both the shocks and clinging of clothing. One is Static Guard, in a spray can using a nonfluorocarbon propellant. The spray is instantly effective on garments, furniture, curtains, carpets, blankets and appliances.

Steam Radiators: In a home with steam heating, certain rooms may get the heat too slowly, or remain always chilly. Balancing the radiator air valves overcomes this. Steam enters the radiator as its valve releases the air. Some valves have different size openings, others are adjustable. The radiators closest to the steam boiler get the smallest-size vent; the chilly ones farther away get the largest vents. Adjust the openings, or switch the valves, so that the desired balance is achieved.

(Caution: Never leave a radiator without its air valve—escaping steam from an open radiator can be lethal. Valves last almost indefinitely if not damaged by impact or clogged by sediment.)

Sterilizing: Medical instruments, such as syringes, tweezers and cutting implements, can be sterilized at home by boiling in clean water for 5 to 10 minutes. The tongs with which the instruments are lifted out also must be sterilized to avoid contamination. Use distilled water or rainwater if available, as tap water may leave a precipitate from its mineral content after boiling, although the precipitate can be removed with vinegar on a cotton pad.

For instant sterilizing of the skin, swab with a cotton ball dipped in 91 percent isopropyl or 70 percent ethyl alcohol, or a foil-wrapped alcohol sterilizing pad. Do not use bathing, rubbing or medicated alcohol for sterilizing.

Boiling is the most dependable method for sanitizing clothing and linens used by a person with a contagious disease, but facilities for tub boiling are no longer available in most homes.

While ordinary laundering in the washing machine may not be sufficient for sanitizing, suitable disinfectants that are harmless to fabrics and dyes can be added. One cup of liquid chlorine bleach in the wash water is an effective bacteria killer, but should not be used on woolens or other fabrics that might be affected. A cupful of Pine-Sol in a top-loading machine will be very effective. But make sure the wash water is really hot, at least 140 degrees, adding boiling water from the stove if necessary.

Sticky Drawers. See *Drawers,* page 71.

Suede: Stroke with a fine bronze-wire brush to remove dirt and
raise the nap. Some light soil can be cleaned with a soap
eraser, but grease spots require sponging with benzene or
other solvent. Another treatment for greasy or compacted
nap is a poultice of sawdust and fuller's earth, moistened with
benzene and allowed to stand on the stain, then brushed off
when dry. Nothing helps, however, when the nap has been
worn down to the leather.
    Commercial cleaners utilize a grit-free powder in a soft,
porous pad (Suede-Mate, Suede Saver). Squeeze the pad so
some powder sifts through to the surface; rub over the soiled
spot. (See *Leather,* page 102.)

Swimming Pools: A combination of water filtration, chemical
treatment, manual skimming and vacuum cleaning keeps
the pool suitable for use.
    Automatic filtering equipment should be of adequate ca-
pacity to pump the entire pool volume every few hours. If
you need to know the volume of water in your pool to select
the proper filter, determine its size in cubic feet and com-
pute 7½ gallons of water per cubic foot; thus a pool 30 feet
by 12 feet with average 4-foot depth, will have 1440 cubic
feet and contain approximately 10,000 gallons, so that a filter
with a flow of 2,000 gallons per hour will circulate the entire
pool contents almost 5 times a day if the filter is left working
around the clock.
    Chemical control is no longer a complex chore, with all-
in-one powders or tablets that combine a balanced proportion of chlorine and algaecides. Daily testing of the water
takes just a moment or two, is essential to assure that the pool
is safe for swimming.
    A hand skimmer with a pole long enough to reach halfway
across the pool has a butterfly net to scoop up leaves and
other debris. An outflow strainer traps twigs, bugs, hair, etc.
—and must be emptied daily.
    Filters require frequent backwashing to clear out sedi-
ment from the filtering sand or cartridge.
    Windblown sand and dirt settling in the bottom of the pool

give it a dirty appearance. A pool vacuum with a long hose that has a large plastic cup at one end to reach the pool bottom sucks up the foreign matter, leaving the water sparkling clear. A large tufted brush fits on the vacuum tube to scrub away any dirt on the pool sides. The vacuum hose is attached to the filter intake hose. The filter also can pump out the entire pool in a few hours for cleaning, repairs and winterizing.

Tape Recorder, Player: Each time a tape cassette is played, a bit of zinc oxide is shed and becomes coated on the mechanism. If left to accumulate, the abrasive crust can result in erratic performance. This condition can be avoided by regular cleaning of the stereo guide bracket, capstans and playback head. Use an extra long cotton swab, moistened with 70 percent isopropyl alcohol. Do not use "rubbing alcohol," which contains glycerine, or any petroleum-base solvent that may damage rubber components.

Car tape decks perform better when cleaned after each 12 hours of use. Demagnetize the heads and other ferrous parts after abot t 4 hours of play to eliminate hissing sounds.

Teflon Cookware: See *Cookware: Teflon-Coated,* page 61.

Telephone: Routine wiping of the exterior surfaces with a damp cloth or sponge and soap is all that is necessary to keep a telephone instrument clean. That is the recommendation of the Bell System, which advises against using chemically treated cloths and harsh detergents, which are harmful to the plastic surface.

It's a fact, however, that food or dirt may become encrusted inside the speaker or receiver perforations, resulting in unpleasant odors. While AT&T emphasizes that the telephone is not considered a source of transmitting infections, even in publicly used instruments, the company says that it desires to make its equipment both attractive and pleasant for its subscribers, so offers to clean and deodorize, or replace without charge, any set that requires this attention.

Television Screen: There is no reason to view your favorite programs through a film of dust on your TV screen. A wipe with a soft dustcloth usually clears it up, but if the plastic facing of your TV set has a grimy coating, use a soft cloth moistened slightly with denatured alcohol or other anti-static cleaner.

Cleaning solutions are sold at television and phonograph record stores. One acceptable brand is Tele-Clear.

Tennis Balls: Brush off dirt or mud, being careful not to damage the nap, which must remain uniform throughout. Shoe whiting is sometimes used to clean smudged tennis balls. Avid players say that to restore balls that have lost their bounce, wrap in aluminum foil, leave in oven at 200 degrees for 20 minutes, and they'll be fit again for about 15 bouncy games.

Tinned Cookware: See *Cookware: Tinned,* page 63.

Toilets: Automatically dispensed with each flushing, blue-dyed, lemon-scented in-tank detergents help keep the vitreous china bowl clean and free of hard-water stains. Occasional swabbing of the bowl with a toilet cleaner, which usually contains chlorine bleach, is necessary. Wash the outside of the bowl and the seat with a sponge and warm sudsy water. Do not use scouring powder on the porcelain bowl.

A bowl swab-brush need not be ugly or unwieldy—a well-designed and even decorative storing caddy keeps it out of sight. Keep the seat cover down to prevent objects like a cake of soap, hairbrush or medicine containers from falling into the bowl. If flushed away, these articles become jammed in the drainpipe and prevent waste flow; usually they require expensive servicing to correct.

Trash Cans: Plastic liners help keep garbage cans clean with minimum effort. Place garbage in closed plastic bags, dispose of promptly. Rinse the cans regularly with the garden hose, adding a little ammonia or chlorine bleach to the rinse water.

Drain the water by upturning; leave cans open to dry. Use well-fitted covers for sanitation and cleanliness.

Trisodium Phosphate (TSP): This strong, general-purpose cleaner, the prime ingredient of many brands of wall and floor detergents (Soilax, Spic and Span, Wilmor) is used also for numerous other purposes around the home. TSP acts by emulsifying grease-bound dirt into tiny particles that are washed away. A small quantity does it—just 1 or 2 table-spoons in 1 gallon of water make a solution for most jobs; the addition of washing soda to the solution extends its effectiveness.

As a wall and floor cleaner, TSP removes wax and washes linoleum, vinyl tiles, marble and terrazzo surfaces. Use 2 to 4 tablespoons in 1 gallon of hot water. This is not for wood floors, which should not be washed with water. Avoid letting the solution run onto painted woodwork, as the TSP can soften the paint, and is used by painters for that purpose.

In laundering, TSP serves as a water softener, so less detergent is needed, and also as a prewash to loosen grease stains. TSP is used in the electrolytic cleaning of silver, boiled in an aluminum pan. (See *Silver,* page 153.)

This chemical is effective for flushing out clogged auto radiators, washing dentures, softening and cleaning paintbrushes, brightening refrigerator, oven, range surfaces and countertops. (Refer to the individual items for details.)

Typewriter: Clean type provides neater letters. The easiest way to clean the type is with a puttylike soft plastic, pressed lightly onto the type faces, that picks up residual ink that clogs the type (Star Type Cleaner).

The use of benzene and other solvents for cleaning may damage the rubber or painted parts of the typewriter. Alcohol is suitable for this purpose—moisten a cloth slightly, stroke the keys so that no fluid drips between them, wipe the surface dry. This method, though, is not so dependable for removing impacted carbon from the type.

The paper platen on most typewriters can be removed for cleaning by lifting the end clamp bars. Wash the rubber platen with soap and warm water, dry and replace. Do not use solvent on the platen as it will soften the rubber.

A little sewing-machine oil on the runners of manual machines helps the carriage move smoothly.

If your fingers become smeared when putting in a new ribbon, a hand soap (Lava, Gresolvent) should do an adequate cleanup, or if your skin is sensitive, rub with a liquid detergent, then wash thoroughly with soap. If traces of the stain remain, wipe with lemon juice.

Umbrella: Open a wet umbrella after you come indoors, leaving it in the bathtub to dry. Make certain the umbrella has dried out properly before you fold it, to avoid mildew and damage to the fabric.

Don't wait for a storm to check out your umbrella. Open it for inspection to see that the catch works smoothly and that all ribs are in place. If a plastic tip has loosened, or a rib slipped its moorings, just a touch of household cement will put it right to face another rainy day.

Upholstery: The correct cleaning method for each type of upholstery fabric is shown on a tag or label attached to the furniture. Some fabrics can be washed with the suds of a water-based liquid dishwasher detergent (Ivory, Palmolive). Mix 2 teaspoons of detergent with ½ cup of water in a blender or with an eggbeater in a bowl. Apply the foam to the fabric with a sponge, covering a larger area than the soiled part to avoid leaving rings; rub lightly; rinse with a newly dampened sponge.

Some fabrics can be cleaned only with a water-free solvent such as Energine, Carbona, Renuzit. Use a sponge, working it outward from the soiled spot to avoid causing a discolored ring. Provide ample ventilation.

Vinyl upholstery covering should be sponged weekly with

a mild detergent to remove body oils that could damage the plastic.

As mentioned earlier, it's not advisable to remove the zippered covers from sofa cushions to be laundered separately, as shrinkage will prevent a neat fit when replaced.

Vacuum Bottles: A simple treatment with baking soda will purge stale odors that could affect the taste of the liquids when the bottle is refilled. Sprinkle in 2 tablespoons of baking soda, partly fill the bottle with hot soapy water, shake well, then rinse at least twice with clear water.

Vacuum Cleaner: If there's still such a thing as a "maid of all work," the vacuum cleaner surely earns that identification. The vacuum has remained basically in the same form almost from its beginning, but there have been numerous improvements in function, increased versatility, greater convenience of use and more attractive appearance. Your basic choice is widened now: There are the canister and upright types; the centrally located built-in-the-walls vacuum system; and the large-capacity, wet-dry tank type designed to handle everything from cleaning the chimney and picking up spillover water in the basement to cleaning up the leaves on the lawn, plus every other vacuum cleaning job in between. The large tank is fitted to a dolly on casters, so is easy to move around, and usually a handle permits carrying the unit up and down stairs.

Many modern vacuums are also fitted with a carpet agitator operated by an individual motor that leaves the carpet looking its best. For the popular shag carpeting, there is an attachment with claws that fluff up the nap for deeper cleaning. Use the vacuum also with shampooing and steam-cleaning equipment for the occasional extensive carpet treatment, to restore color and clean out deep-seated dirt.

Occasional attention to maintenance will keep the vacuum

Water Marks: See *Stains: Silk,* page 167 and *Water Spots,* page 168.

Water Pipe—Emergency Repair: Locate point of the leak if you can, then shut off the main valve and open all higher faucets to drain the lines into the lowest fixture. Dry the pipe, cover the leak with sheet rubber (available from a service station where it is used as tube patching) and apply pressure from a C-clamp on the spot. This should hold for a while until repairs can be made.

If the leak comes from a single pinhole, you might try patching with epoxy cement. Scrape clean with sandpaper; press on a small amount of the properly mixed cement with a putty knife or other flat tool. Let the cement set for an hour or more before turning on the water.

Replacing a section of copper tubing is not vey difficult, use either the sweat-soldering method with a propane torch for heating, or a flaring tool and compression fittings to join the new tube section. Cut tube only with a special disk type cutter, not with a hack saw, to assure neat ends for proper coupling of the insert section.

Water Sanitation: The garden hose filling a wading pool on the lawn looks innocent enough, but only to those who do not realize the potential danger of contaminating your home's water supply. A similar situation exists when the garden hose is allowed to remain on the ground or grass when watering the lawn. The hazard results from the siphoning effect that occurs when water pressure drops, even slightly and momentarily. This is easily demonstrated with the garden hose. When a water valve opens anywhere in the house, the water flow from the hose drops, then picks up again. That sudden drop in pressure causes a vacuum that may be sufficient to siphon water back into the system, and with it the toxic bacteria that are always present on the ground. And there's no telling how far this bacterial invasion can go once it gets into the lines.

The solution is a simple device, called an anti-siphon valve or a vacuum breaker, usually made of rubber. It is installed into the water line or at a plumbing fixture. Protection from similar "back-flow" contamination is also provided by plumbing regulations requiring an adequate "air gap" or space between the faucet or other water-supply inlet and the sink bowl.

"Pop-up" lawn sprinklers avoid contamination because the sprinkler head is raised above the lawn when the water pressure goes on, and drops back instantly when the water is turned off.

Water Softener: Laundering and personal washing are affected by hard water, which contains excessive amounts of minerals (mostly calcium, magnesium and iron) which combine chemically with soap to form curds of mineral salt, and reduce the washing effectiveness of detergents so that much greater quantities of the latter are required for washing. Certain chemicals in detergents act as nonprecipitating softeners (Calgon, Spring Rain, etc.). Other water softeners precipitate and suspend the minerals in the wash water to prevent formation of scum.

Homeowners in hard-water areas can obtain from their local water department or the water-supply company the necessary information regarding degree of hardness, and recommendations on the chemical treatment necessary to soften the water. The basic chemicals used are sal soda, borax, trisodium phosphate (TSP) and ammonia. The correct quantity of softening agent is a critical detail, since the addition of too much washing soda renders the water supply excessively alkaline, while an insufficient quantity of softening agent fails to achieve the necessary result.

Whitewall Tires: See *Automobile Cleaning,* page 37.

Whitewash: Often seen in older homes as the chalk-white coating on fences, barns, tree trunks and interior foundation walls, it is known also as calcimine, although the formulas are somewhat different. While whitewash consists basically of quicklime (calcium hydroxide), it is sometimes constituted with casein for weather resistance and durability.

Whitewash does not itself take too well to washing, but as the name denotes, it serves the function of brightening surfaces that otherwise would not lend themselves to cleaning methods, particularly rough exterior structures. The inexpensive, easy to apply whitewash coating produces a fresh, clean-looking surface. Before renewing a whitewashed surface, all flaking and peeling areas must be scraped or scrubbed away. If the surface is to be coated with an oil or latex paint, all the old whitewash or calcimine must be removed to provide a good base. In some instances, this can be done only by sandblasting.

Wickerware. See *Furniture: Wickerware,* page 83.

Window Screens: The best place to wash screens is outdoors on the lawn or driveway, spraying with the garden hose. Repair and wash screens each year before installing them for the season. (see *Screens,* page 149.)

Set up the screens for washing at an angle against a fence or other support. Use a pailful of warm water with detergent; scrub screens and their frames with a soft-bristle brush. Rinse with spray from the garden hose or by splashing pails of clean water against the screen. Allow to air-dry. Copper or bronze screening cloth will be more attractive and will last much longer if coated with clear lacquer from an aerosol can.

If necessary to wash screens indoors, the best place is on the floor in the basement or garage, near a floor drain. Another possibility is the bathtub, but be sure to line the tub with old towels to prevent scratching the porcelain; lay newspapers thickly outside the tub to absorb splashed water.

Window Shades: Most shade cloth can be cleaned and kept fresh looking without taking down the shade by occasional dusting, vacuuming, or wiping with a damp cloth. Vertical blinds also are cleaned the same easy way. Cloth shades that are not washable can be refreshed with a wallpaper cleaner, or in the case of a few soft-textured styles, professionally dry-cleaned. When purchasing shades, make your selection after checking to see which cleaning method is recommended.

For a complete spring or fall cleaning job, a few simple

steps will rejuvenate your washable shades. Take down the shades, one by one. Spread each shade on a large table and wash it section by section, with a sudsy cloth or sponge, starting at the top near the roller, using as little water as possible. Avoid letting water flow on and streak the unwashed parts of the shade. "Damp rinse" and dry each section as it is done. When completed, reverse the shade and repeat the process on the other side.

Hang the open shade full-length at the window until thoroughly dry; then take the shade down again, roll it up tightly and replace in the roller brackets. Leave it rolled up for about 12 hours. This simple "roll-up" trick leaves the shade material perfectly flat.

When a shade roller snaps around on its bracket, losing spring tension so that it balks at being raised, lift the roller out of its brackets. One end has a projecting flat bar to fit a slotted bracket; at the other end a pin fits into a hole on the other bracket. Roll up the shade tightly, slip the ends into the proper brackets. The spring tension is automatically restored as the shade is pulled down.

ROMAN WINDOW SHADES: Vacuum lightly to clean; avoid pulling the woven threads out of place. Spray on Scotchgard coating to protect the weave against oily stains which would be difficult to remove.

VINYL SLAT SHADES: Lower the shade, wipe slats on both sides, including the valance, with a soapy cloth.

Windshield: See *Automobile Cleaning,* page 37.

Window Washing: Many products and methods are available for cleaning windows, all quite efficient and each with its devoted supporters. Professional window washers, who should know best, just brush on clear water and dry with a rubber squeegee, wiping the rubber edge after each stroke with a chamois.

Favored by homemakers are vinegar, alcohol, kerosene, borax, ammonia, various detergents and talc. Popular commercial cleaners are Windex, Glass Wax, Glass Plus and Bon Ami.

A mop on a long handle, dipped into a pail of water, is a convenient way to wash the outside of a picture window. The main problem is reaching into the corners, which can best be done with a small brush or a cotton swab if the corners can be reached directly. Inspect each window when done for residual streaks, polish with a soft cloth, dry chamois, paper towel or newsprint paper.

If you wash windows when there is a likelihood of freezing weather, add 2 tablespoons of glycerine (from the drugstore) or rubbing alcohol to both wash- and rinse-water. A film will remain on the glass to keep it from icing or steaming up. It's best not to wash windows on a hot day when the sun is shining right on them, as the glass will dry too fast and look streaked. Don't forget to wipe the windowsills dry when you're done. Replace any screens and shades that have been taken down.

Wood Floors: See *Floors: Wood,* page 79.

Wok: Whether your wok is of aluminum, carbon steel or porcelain enamel on steel, avoid changes in temperature that may cause the metal to warp. Remove heat control before immersing an electric wok in water. Use only a plastic or wooden non-stick stirrer. Never cut food inside a non-stick wok.

Clean the fired-on non-stick interior finish thoroughly with a plastic pad such as Scotch-Brite to be sure there is no residual layer of food or grease which will carbonize when reheated, resulting in stains that are difficult to remove. Do not use a metal scouring pad or harsh scouring powder on either type of finish. Clean the porcelain exterior finish and the phenolic trim on the cover with hot soapy water and a soft sponge.

Part Three
Sources of Further
Information

Keep Those Booklets

Save the instruction booklets that come with the appliances and equipment you buy for your home. The information in them will help you get the best, most carefree and most economical service. File booklets and instruction sheets all together in a folder or box so they can be located readily when needed, often years later. While the appliances are still new, write the model and serial numbers, the date and place of purchase, and other relevant data regarding the appliances, directly in the pertinent booklets. Nearly always there are directions on how to find the serial numbers and model numbers.

Instructions in these booklets often affect the guarantee, such as cautions against dismantling certain parts, or cleaning with steel wool which can damage an enameled coating and invalidate the guarantee.

Refer to the instruction booklet when you have difficulty removing a refrigerator shelf, or reaching some part for replacement; often just a simple catch or button does the trick, whereas frustrated attempts to apply force can be destructive. If a sketch of the assembly is provided, you will be better able to figure out the proper operation of the equipment or how to make repairs.

These booklets do not always present the needed information in a comprehensible manner, and certain important procedures may be entirely omitted, deliberately or not. However, the booklet will provide you with the manufacturer's name and location; do not hesitate to write, requesting any information you require, including the source of replacement parts not available locally. Most reputable firms are eager to assist consumers. Many have special customer-service departments, and you may be agreeably surprised by the cooperation that you receive.

Much information and practical literature is available, often just for the writing or at nominal cost. Following are booklets available from a number of sources, for which you may wish to write:

Available from the U.S. Department of Agriculture, Washington, D.C. 20250:

"Removing Stains from Fabrics." Home and Garden Bulletin No. 62.   Free

"Soaps and Detergents for Home Laundering." Home and Garden Bulletin No. 139.   Free

"Sanitation in Home Laundering." Home and Garden Bulletin No. 97.   Free

"Be Safe from Insects in Recreational Areas." Home and Garden Bulletin No. 200.   10 cents

Available from Consumer Information Service, Public Documents Distribution Center, Pueblo, Col. 81009:

"Look for That Label." No. 039A. 1971.   Free

"Vacuum Cleaners: Their Selection, Use and Care." 1972. 60 cents

"Dishwashers." 1972.   70 cents

"Washers and Dryers." 1972.   45 cents

"Manual of Septic Tank Practice." Public Health Service Manual No. 526.   40 cents

"Clothing and Fabric Care; Labeling." No. 036A. 1972. Free

Available from the Federal Trade Commission, 6th and Pennsylvania Avenue NW, Washington, D.C. 20580:

"Care and Labeling of Textile Wearing Apparel." Free

Available from Dan River Mills, Inc., Public Relations, P.O. Box 6126, Station B, Greenville, S.C. 29606:

"A Dictionary of Textile Terms," 11th ed. Free

Available from the Superintendent of Documents, U.S. Government Printing Office, Washington, D.C. 20402:

"Fibers and Fabrics." N.B.S. Consumer Information Series. No. 1970   65 cents

"First Aid for Flooded Homes." Agriculture Handbook No. 38.   20 cents

"Exterior Painting, Home and Garden." USDA Bulletin N. 155.   10 cents

"Interior Painting in Homes." Home and Garden Bulletin No. 184.   10 cents

"Simple Home Repairs—Inside!" Extension Service Program Aid No. 1034.   40 cents·

"Vacuum Cleaners." General Services Administration Publication No. 1072.   40 cents

"Ants in the Home and Garden." USDA Home and Garden Bulletin No. 28.   10 cents

"Protecting Woolens Against Clothes Moths and Carpet Beetles." USDA Home and Garden Bulletin No. 113.   20 cents

"How to Prevent and Remove Mildew: Home Methods." USDA Home and Garden Bulletin No. 68.   Free

Other Information Materials Available from:

Armour-Dial, Inc., Phoenix, Ariz. 85077: "Parsons' Household Cleaning Wall Chart." Chart shows uses of ammonia for various household cleaning purposes, including correct applications and safety precautions.

Armstrong Cork Co., Lancaster, Pa. 17604: "How to Keep Floor Covering Looking Its Best." Pamphlet. Free.

A. Beshar & Co., 49 East 53rd St., New York, N.Y. 10022: "Aids to Interior Decor Fabric Care." Pamphlet. Free.

Johnson Wax, Consumer Education Dept., Box 567, Racine, Wis. 53403: "Furniture Care," "Rug and Carpet Care" and "Floor Care." Pamphlets. All free.

National Paint, Varnish and Lacquer Association, Inc., 1500 Rhode Island Ave. NW, Washington, D.C. 20005: "Guides to Selecting, Applying and Cleaning Paint for Home Purposes."

RIT Consumer Service Laboratory, Best Foods Division, CPC International, 1437 West Morris St., Indianapolis, Ind. 46206: "Tie-Dye and Dip-Dye Instructions." Free.

Scott's Liquid Gold, Box 7192, Denver, Col. 80207: "For Love of Wood." Free.

Soap and Detergent Association, 475 Park Ave., New York, N.Y. 10016: "Housekeeping Directors." Free.

Tile Council of America, P.O. Box 2222, Dept. WDIY, Princeton, N.J. 08540: "Guide to Installing Ceramic Tile on Walls of Bathrooms and Kitchens." Contains step-by-step instructions and a number of beautiful room settings in full color. Leaflet. 25 cents.

Part Four
Sources of
Products

There are an almost infinite number of products for cleaning purposes, and new ones are introduced nearly every day —or so it seems. Brand-name products are mentioned in this book for identification only and as a convenience to readers, not necessarily as a recommendation to the exclusion of similar products. While most of the listed items are readily available at the usual sources, the manufacturers and their addresses are supplied here for reference:

A

Acrilon 45	DuPont Co. Wilmington, Del. 19898
Ajax Cleanser	Colgate-Palmolive Co. New York, N.Y. 10016
all	Lever Bros. 390 Park Ave. New York, N.Y. 10017
Alumi-Nu Cleaner	Alumni-Nu Co. 4200 Lee Rd. Cleveland, Ohio 44128
Anti-Fog	Merix Chemical Co. 2234 E. 75 St. Chicago, Ill. 60649

Anti-Static for Records

Merix Chemical Co.
2234 E. 75 St.
Chicago, Ill. 60649

Arm & Hammer Detergent

Church & Dwight Co.
2 Pennsylvania Plaza
New York, N.Y. 10001

Arrow Squeegee

Ardmore Co.
3445 N. Western Ave.
Chicago, Ill. 60618

b

Beacon Floor Wax
  (Self-Polishing)

Lehn & Fink Co.
Montvale, N.J. 07645

Bon Ami Cleaner & Polisher

Faultless Starch Bon
Ami Co.
1025 W. 8 St.
Kansas City, Mo. 64101

Brasso Polisher

R. T. French Co.
1 Mustard St.
Rochester, N.Y. 14609

c

Cameo Copper Cleaner

Purex Co.
Lakewood, Calif. 90712

Carbona Spot Lifter

Carbona Products
30–50 Greenpoint Ave.
Long Island City, N.Y.
11101

Carpet Shock Free
(for Static Electricity)

Magic American
23700 Mercantile Ave.
Cleveland, Ohio 44122

Chore Girl/Chore Boy

Metal Textile Co.
P. O. Box 315
S. Bound Brook, N.J.
08880

Clorox	Clorox Co. Oakland, Calif. 94612
Copper-Brite Cleaner	Copper Brite, Inc. 5147 West Jefferson Blvd. Los Angeles, Calif. 90016
Corningware	Corning Glassworks Corning, N.Y. 14830

d

Dacron Polyester	DuPont Co. Wilmington, Del. 19898
Damp Rid	Vapor Products P. O. Box 8294 Orlando, Fla. 32806
Dap	Dap, Inc. P. O. Box 277 Dayton, Ohio 45401
Dekro Lucite Cleaner	Beaver Laboratory 5100 W. Commercial St. Tamarac, Fla. 33319
Dentu-Creme	Block Drug Co. Newark, N.J. 07302
Deruto	Dap, Inc. Dayton, Ohio 45401
Devcon Silicone Spray	Devcon Corp. Danvers, Mass. 01923
Dico Buffing Kit (for Brass, Aluminum, Silver)	Divine Brothers Co. 200 Seward Ave. Utica, N.Y. 13503
Dip-It	Economics Laboratories St. Paul, Minn. 55102
Dow Adhesives	Dow Corning Co. Midland, Mich.

Dremel Handy Kit	Dremel Co. 4915 21st St. Racine, Wis. 53406
Duro De-Greaser	Woodhull Chemical Co. 18731 Cranwood Parkway Cleveland, Ohio 44128

E

Easy-Off Wallpaper Remover	Kleen-Strip Co. P. O. Box 1879 Memphis, Tenn. 38101
Electrosol Dishwasher Detergent	Economics Laboratories St. Paul, Minn. 55102

f

Fantastik Detergent	Texize Chemical Co. P. O. Box 368 Greenville, S.C. 29602
Fast Wallpaper Remover	Savogran Co. 259 Lenox St. Norwood, Mass. 02062
Final Touch Fabric Softener	Lever Bros. Co. 390 Park Ave. New York, N.Y. 10017
Flex-O-Glaze Acrylic	Warp Bros. Chicago, Ill. 60651
Florco Driveway Cleaner	Floridin Co. 3 Penn Center Pittsburgh, Pa. 15235
Foamy Dish Detergent	Industrial Equities San Galte, Calif. 90280
4X Ignition Spray	Dow Corning Co. Midland, Mich. 48640

G

Garage Magic	Magic American 23700 Mercantile Ave. Cleveland, Ohio 44122
Glass Wax	Gold Seal Co. 210 N. 4 St. Bismarck, N.Dak. 58501
Glory Foam Rug Cleaner	S. J. Johnson & Son Racine, Wis. 53403
Goddard Jewelry Cleaner	J. Goddard & Sons P.O. Box 808 Manitowoc, Wis. 54220
Groom Upholstery Cleaner	Westley Industries 1898 Scranton Rd. Cleveland, Ohio 44128
Gunk Swab and Engine Cleaner	Gunk Laboratory 5829 W. 66 St. Chicago, Ill. 60638

H

Heddy Exhaust Fan	Heddy Corp. 100 6th Ave. Paterson, N.J. 07524
Heet Auto Engine Cleaner	DeMert & Dougherty Co. 5000 W. 41 St. Chicago, Ill. 60650
Henkel Wallpaper Remover	Henkel, Inc. Teaneck, N.J. 07666
Hunter Exhaust Fan	Robbins & Meyers Co. 2500 Frisco Ave. Memphis, Tenn. 38114

i

Instant Coffeepot Cleaner

Revere Copper Co.
260 Park Ave.
New York, N.Y. 10017

j

Jet-Dry for Glassware

Economics Laboratories
St. Paul, Minn. 55102

Jewel Clean

W.J.Hagerty & Sons
P. O. Box 1496
South Bend, Ind. 46624

Johnson's Wax

Johnson Products
2072 N. Commerce St.
Milwaukee, Wis. 53212

Jolastie Washing Solution

Jobst Instutute
P.O. Box 653
Toledo, Ohio 43694

k

K2r Spot Lifter

Texize Chemical Co.
P.O. Box 368
Greenville, S.C. 29602

Kleen Strip Wallpaper Remover

Kleen-Strip Co.
P.O. Box 1879
Memphis, Tenn. 38101

Kodak Lens Cleaner

Eastman Kodak Co.
Rochester, N.Y. 14660

Kozak Auto Body Cloths

Kozak Co.
18 South Lyon St.
Batavia, N.Y. 14020

Krazy Glue

Krazy Glue Co.
53 W. 23 St.
New York, N.Y. 10010

l

Lanol White Shoe Cleaner	Esquire Polishes Jamaica N.Y. 11434
Lexan Acrilic	General Electric Co. 14 Commerce Dr. Cranford, N.J. 07016
Liquid Gold	Scott's, Inc. 4880 Havana St. Denver, Colo. 80239
Loctite Glue	Loctite Co. 705 N. Mountain Rd. Newington, Conn 06111
Lysol Disinfectant	Lehn & Fink Montvale, N.J. 07645

M

Magic Copper Cleaner	Magic American 23700 Mercantile Ave. Cleveland, Ohio 44122
Marble Magic	Magic American 23700 Mercantile Ave. Cleveland, Ohio 441226
Minute Bond Adhesive	Loctite Co. 705 N. Mountain Rd. Newington, Conn. 06111
Mirro Metal Polish	Mirro Aluminum Co. Manitowoc, Wis. 54220
Mop and Glo	Lehn & Fink Montvale, N.J. 07645

N

Naval Jelly	Woodhall Chemical Co. 18731 Cranwood Pkwy. Cleveland, Ohio 44128

No Flame Paint Remover

Reliable Paste Co.
3560 Shields Ave.
Chicago, Ill. 60609

Noxon Metal Polish

Boyle-Midway Co.
American Home
  Products Co.
685 Third Ave.
New York, N.Y. 10017

NuTone Exhaust Fans

NuTone Division
Scovill Co.
Madison St. at Red
  Bank St.
Cincinnati, Ohio 45227

O

On the Ball Golfball Cleaner

Merix Co.
2234 E. 75 St.
Chicago, Ill. 60649

One-Wipe Dust Cloth

J. Parmet Co.
Catasauqua, Pa. 18032

Orlon Acrylic

DuPont Co.
Wilmington, Del. 19898

P

Parsons' Ammonia

Armour-Dial Co.
Phoenix, Ariz. 85077

Pine Sol Detergent

American Cyanamid Co.
Wayne, N.J. 07470

Pledge Wood Polish

S.J. Johnson & Sons
Racine, Wis. 53403

Pro-Tek Hand Cleaner

DuPont Co.
Wilmington, Del. 19898

R

Rain Dance Auto Polishes	DuPont Co. Wilmington, Del. 19898
Rally Auto Products	DuPont Co. Wilmington, Del. 19898
Renuzit Cleaner	Drackett Co. 5020 Spring Grove Ave. Cincinnati, Ohio 45232
Rescue Soap Pads	3-M Company St. Paul, Minn. 55101
Rubgum	Durasol Drug Co. Amesbury, Mass. 01913
Rust-Oleum	Rust-Oleum Corp. 2301 Oakton Evanston, Ill. 60204

S

Saddlers Wax	J. Goddard & Sons P.O. Box 808 Manitowoc, Wis. 54220
SAR Lucite	DuPont Co. Wilmington, Del. 19898
Savogran Cleaner	Savogran Co. 256 Lenox St. Norwood, Mass. 02062
Scotchgard	3M Co. St. Paul, Minn. 55101
Shade Safe	Durasol Drug Co., Amesbury, Mass. 01913
Shepherd Casters	Shepherd Co. 203 Kerth St. St. Joseph, Mo. 49085

Shower-Dri Squeegee	Greenview Mfg. Co. 2557 Greenview St. Chicago, Ill. 60614
Simonize Wax and Cleaner	S.J. Johnson & Son Racine, Wis. 53403
Slide-All Lubricant	Elmer's Division Bordens, Inc. Columbus, Ohio 43215
Snoopy Lectric Comb	Kenner Products 1014 Vine St. Cincinnati, Ohio 45202
SnoShoo (for white shoes)	Dow Corning Co. Midland, Mich. 48640
Soilax	Economics Laboratories St. Paul, Minn. 55102
Solarian Floor Finish	Armstrong Cork Co. Lancaster, Pa. 17604
Solvents (various types)	National Solvent Co. Medina, Ohio 44256
Sparkle Safe Crystal Cleaner	Sparkle Safe, Inc. 1501 Boston Post Rd. Milford, Conn. 06460
Speedhide Wall Sealer	P.P.G. Industries Pittsburgh, Pa.
Sprayway Glass Cleaner	Sprayway, Inc. 484 Vista Ave. Addison, Ill. 60101
Squirt Windshield De-icer	Merix Chemical 2234 E. 75 St. Chacago, Ill. 606101
Star Typewriter Cleaner	Eberhard Faber Co. Crestwood Park Wilkes-Barre, Pa. 18703
Sudbury Gel Coat	Sudbury Laboratories Sudbury, Mass 01776

Suede Saver	Kiwi Polish Co. 2 High St. Pottstown, Pa. 19464
Super Glue	Woodhill Chemical Cleveland, Ohio 44128

T

Teflon	DuPont Co. Wilmington, Del. 19898
Tile & Grout Magic	Magic American 23700 Mercantile Ave. Cleveland, Ohio 44122
Turtle Wax	Turtle Wax Co. 5655 W. 73 St. Chicago, Ill. 60638
TV Tele-Clear	Merix Chemical 2234 E. 75 St. Chicago, Ill. 60649
20-Mule Team Borax	U.S. Borax & Chemical Co. 3075 Wilshire Blvd. Los Angeles, Calif. 90010
Twinkle Copper Cleaner	Drackett Co. 5020 Spring Grove Ave. Cincinnati, Ohio 45232

W

Walltex Vinyl Wallcovering	Columbus Coated Fabrics 180 E. Broad St. Columbus, Ohio 43215
Wantz Coffeemaker Cleaner	Illinois Water Treat- ment Co. Rockford, Ill. 61105
WD-40 Lubricant	WD-40 Co. 1061 Cudahy Pl. San Diego, Calif. 92110

Wet-or-Dry Sandpaper	3-M Co. St. Paul, Minn. 55101
Whisk-Away Rust Remover	W. T. Stewart Co. Sedalia, Mo. 65301
Wilmor TSP	Willis-Moore Co. 4702 E. 50 St. Los Angeles, Cal. 90058
Wisk	Lever Bros. 390 Park Ave. New York, N.Y. 10017
Wonder Water Wash Paint Remover	Wilson Imperial Co. 115 Chestnut St. Newark, N.J. 07105

X

X-14 Mildew Remover	White Laboratories P.O. Box 15335 Orlando, Fla. 32808

ABOUT THE AUTHOR

One of America's most successful writers on home maintenance and workshop subjects, Ralph Treves began his career
as a newspaper reporter and editor and has had a lifelong
interest in mechanics and woodworking. He was associated
with McGraw-Hill as crafts editor, then wrote the weekly
Handyman feature for the *Philadelphia Inquirer* and the
Los Angeles Times. He is author of nearly a dozen books,
hundreds of magazine articles and numerous instruction
booklets on manual skills and the use of tools. His articles
have appeared in *Popular Science, Popular Mechanics,
Workbench, Better Homes and Gardens, Time-Life Books,
Mechanix Illustrated* and other publications.

Ralph Treves is past president of the National Association
of Home Workshop Writers and a member of the National
Association of Science Writers. His home is in Florida.